First World War
and Army of Occupation
War Diary
France, Belgium and Germany

23 DIVISION
69 Infantry Brigade
Alexandra, Princess of Wales's Own (Yorkshire Regiment)
9th Battalion
23 August 1915 - 31 October 1917

WO95/2184/3

The Naval & Military Press Ltd
www.nmarchive.com
Published in association with The National Archives

Published by

The Naval & Military Press Ltd

Unit 10 Ridgewood Industrial Park,

Uckfield, East Sussex,

TN22 5QE England

Tel: +44 (0) 1825 749494

www.naval-military-press.com

www.nmarchive.com

This diary has been reprinted in facsimile from the original. Any imperfections are inevitably reproduced and the quality may fall short of modern type and cartographic standards.

© Crown Copyright
Images reproduced by permission of The National Archives, London, England, 2015.

Contents

Document type	Place/Title	Date From	Date To
Heading	WO95/2184/3. 9th Btn Yorks 1915 Aug-1917 Oct		
Heading	23rd Division 69th Infy Bde 9th Bn Yorkshire Regt Aug 1915-1917 Oct To Italy		
Miscellaneous			
Heading	23rd Division 9th Yorkshire Regt. Vol I From 23-31.8.15		
War Diary	Bramshott	23/08/1915	26/08/1915
War Diary	Boulogne	27/08/1915	27/08/1915
War Diary	Watten	28/08/1915	28/08/1915
War Diary	Mentque Nortbecourt	28/08/1915	31/08/1915
Heading	23rd Division 9th Yorkshires Vol 2 Sept. 15		
Heading	War Diary Of 9th Yorks Regt. From 1st September to 30th September 1915 inclusive Vol 2		
War Diary	Norbecourt	01/09/1915	06/09/1915
War Diary	Wallons Sur Capel	07/09/1915	07/09/1915
War Diary	Vieux Berquin	08/09/1915	09/09/1915
War Diary	Rue Del Pierre	10/09/1915	12/09/1915
War Diary	Vieux Berquin	13/09/1915	15/09/1915
War Diary	Rue De Biez	16/09/1915	30/09/1915
Heading	23rd Division 9th Yorkshire Regt. Vol 3 Oct 15		
War Diary	War Diary Of 9th Yorks Regt. From 1st October To 31st October 1915 Inclusive Vol: 3		
War Diary	Bois Grenier Line	01/10/1915	02/10/1915
War Diary	L'Hallobeau	03/10/1915	03/10/1915
War Diary	Estaires	04/10/1915	11/10/1915
War Diary	Fort Rompu	11/10/1915	11/10/1915
War Diary	Ruemarle	14/10/1915	15/10/1915
War Diary	Trenches	15/10/1915	24/10/1915
War Diary	Trenches.	23/10/1915	23/10/1915
War Diary	Rue Marle	24/10/1915	30/10/1915
Heading	23rd Division 9th Yorkshire Vol. 4 Nov 15		
Heading	War Diary Of 9th Yorks Regiment From 1st To 30th November 1915 (Inclusive) Volume 4		
War Diary	Rue Marle.	01/11/1915	05/11/1915
War Diary	T 59. 60.61. 62	06/11/1915	10/11/1915
War Diary	Boisgrenier Line	18/11/1915	18/11/1915
War Diary	Rue Marle	21/11/1915	21/11/1915
War Diary	T 57. 58. 59 60 T 61	24/11/1917	24/11/1917
War Diary	Fort Rompu	25/11/1915	30/11/1915
Heading	War Diary Of 9th Yorkshire Regiment From 1st December 1915 To 31st December 1915 (Volume V).		
War Diary	Fort Rompu	01/12/1915	06/12/1915
War Diary	Rue Delettree	06/12/1915	10/12/1915
War Diary	T 47. 48. 49. 50. 51	10/12/1915	14/12/1915
War Diary	Rue Delettree	14/12/1915	18/12/1915
War Diary	T 47.48.49.50.51	18/12/1915	22/12/1915
War Diary	L'Hallobeau	22/12/1915	29/12/1915
War Diary	T.62.63.64.65.66	29/12/1915	31/12/1915
Heading	War Diary Of 9th Yorkshire Regiment. From 1st January 1916 To 31st January 1916 (Inclusive) Vol 6		

War Diary	T 16.1 To T 21.2	01/01/1916	01/01/1916
War Diary	Rue Marle	02/01/1916	02/01/1916
War Diary	I 16. 1 to I 21.2	06/01/1916	06/01/1916
War Diary	Rue Marle	10/01/1916	10/01/1916
War Diary	Rue Dormoire	14/01/1916	14/01/1916
War Diary	I 311 to I 31.5	23/01/1916	27/01/1916
War Diary	Rue Delettree	27/01/1916	27/01/1916
War Diary	I 311 to I 31.5	31/01/1916	31/01/1916
Miscellaneous	First Army No. 502/5 (G) D/-10/1/16	10/01/1916	10/01/1916
Heading	23rd Div. 9th Yorkshire Vol 6		
Heading	War Diary Of 9th Yorkshire Regt. From 1st-29th February 1916. Vol 7		
War Diary	T. I 31.1 To I 31.5	01/02/1916	04/02/1916
War Diary	Rue Delettree	04/02/1916	04/02/1916
War Diary	Jesus Farm	08/02/1916	08/02/1916
War Diary	Vieux Berquin	14/02/1916	14/02/1916
War Diary	Steen Becque	15/02/1916	15/02/1916
War Diary	Estaires	23/02/1916	23/02/1916
War Diary	Steen Becque	27/02/1916	27/02/1916
Heading	War Diary Of 9th Yorkshire Regiment. From 1/3/16 To 31/3/16 Vol 8		
War Diary	Ruitz	01/03/1916	04/03/1916
War Diary	Gouy Servins	04/03/1916	06/03/1916
War Diary	Souchez	06/03/1916	08/03/1916
War Diary	Villers au Bois	10/03/1916	10/03/1916
War Diary	Bois De Bouvigny	14/03/1916	14/03/1916
War Diary	Camblain Chatelain	15/03/1916	15/03/1916
War Diary	Fosse 10	19/03/1916	30/03/1916
Heading	War Diary Of 9th Yorkshire Regiment. From 1st April 1916 To 30th April 1916 Volume IX.		
War Diary	Fosse 10	01/04/1916	04/04/1916
War Diary	Angres	04/04/1916	10/04/1916
War Diary	Fosse 10	10/04/1916	16/04/1916
War Diary	Hersin	16/04/1916	18/04/1916
War Diary	Camblain Chatelain	18/04/1916	19/04/1916
War Diary	Febvin Palfart	19/04/1916	20/04/1916
War Diary	Reclinghem	20/04/1916	25/04/1916
War Diary	Febvin Palfart	25/04/1916	26/04/1916
War Diary	Hersin.	26/04/1916	30/04/1916
Heading	War Diary Of 9th Yorkshire Regt. From 1-5-16 To 31-5-16 Volume 10		
War Diary	Hersin	01/05/1916	01/05/1916
War Diary	Ourton	04/05/1916	04/05/1916
War Diary	Hersin	11/05/1916	11/05/1916
War Diary	Angres 2	12/05/1916	12/05/1916
War Diary	Bully Grenay	17/05/1916	17/05/1916
War Diary	Angres 2	22/05/1916	22/05/1916
War Diary	Fosse 10	26/05/1916	26/05/1916
War Diary	Bully Grenay.	26/05/1916	26/05/1916
War Diary	Verdrel	30/05/1916	30/05/1916
Heading	War Diary Of 9th Yorkshire Regt. From June 1st 1916 To June 30th 1916 (Volume XI).		
War Diary	Verdrel	01/06/1916	01/06/1916
War Diary	Souchezi	09/06/1916	09/06/1916
War Diary	Fosse 10	13/06/1916	13/06/1916
War Diary	Pernes	14/06/1916	14/06/1916

War Diary	Serny	16/06/1916	16/06/1916
War Diary	Longueau	24/06/1916	24/06/1916
War Diary	St Sauveur	25/06/1916	25/06/1916
Heading	69th Inf. Bde. 23rd Div. 9th Battn. The Yorkshire Regiment. July 1916		
Heading	War Diary Of 9th Yorkshire Regt. From July 1st To July 31st 1916 (Volume 12).		
War Diary	St. Sauveur	01/07/1916	01/07/1916
War Diary	Bazieux	01/07/1916	01/07/1916
War Diary	Albert	02/07/1916	02/07/1916
War Diary	Trenches	03/07/1916	05/07/1916
War Diary	Belle Vue Farm	06/07/1916	07/07/1916
War Diary	Trenches	10/07/1916	10/07/1916
War Diary	Belle Vue Farm	12/07/1916	12/07/1916
War Diary	Franvillers	12/07/1916	12/07/1916
War Diary	Molliens Au Bois	13/07/1916	13/07/1916
War Diary	Millen Court	21/07/1916	23/07/1916
War Diary	Albert	26/07/1916	26/07/1916
War Diary	Trenches	28/07/1916	30/07/1916
Heading	69th Brigade. 23rd Division. 1/9th Battalion Yorkshire Regiment August 1916		
Heading	War Diary Of 9th Yorkshire Regt. From August 1st 1916 To August 31st 1916 (Volume 13).		
War Diary	Trenches	01/08/1916	07/08/1916
War Diary	Bresle	08/08/1916	08/08/1916
War Diary	Yaucourt Bussus	11/08/1916	11/08/1916
War Diary	In Train	13/08/1916	13/08/1916
War Diary	Schaexken Nr Berthen	14/08/1916	14/08/1916
War Diary	Steenwerck	17/08/1916	17/08/1916
War Diary	Papot	18/08/1916	18/08/1916
War Diary	Soyer Farm	22/08/1916	22/08/1916
War Diary	Creslow Farm	25/08/1916	31/08/1916
Heading	9th Yorkshire Regt. War Diary. Sept.1916		
Heading	War Diary Of 9th Yorkshire Regt. From Sept. 1st To Sept. 30th 1916 (Volume 14).		
War Diary	Creslow Farm Ploegsteert	01/09/1916	01/09/1916
War Diary	Trenches	02/09/1916	02/09/1916
War Diary	Camp	04/09/1916	04/09/1916
War Diary	Moulle	06/09/1916	06/09/1916
War Diary	Coisy	11/09/1916	11/09/1916
War Diary	Henencourt	12/09/1916	12/09/1916
War Diary	Millen Court	15/09/1916	15/09/1916
War Diary	Trenches	18/09/1916	21/09/1916
War Diary	Div. Reserve	22/09/1916	22/09/1916
War Diary	Brigade Reserve	26/09/1916	26/09/1916
Heading	War Diary Of 9th Yorkshire Regiment. From Oct. 1st 1916 To Oct. 31st 1916 (Volume 15).		
War Diary	Trenches	01/10/1916	07/10/1916
War Diary	Camp	09/10/1916	09/10/1916
War Diary	Albert	09/10/1916	09/10/1916
War Diary	Entraining	12/10/1916	12/10/1916
War Diary	Conteville	13/10/1916	13/10/1916
War Diary	Poperinghe	15/10/1916	15/10/1916
War Diary	Ypres	23/10/1916	26/10/1916
War Diary	Trenches	29/10/1916	01/11/1916
War Diary	Divisional Reserve	04/11/1916	04/11/1916

War Diary	Ypres	10/11/1916	10/11/1916
War Diary	Trenches	16/11/1916	16/11/1916
War Diary	Divisional Reserve	22/11/1916	22/11/1916
War Diary	Ypres	29/11/1916	29/11/1916
Miscellaneous	H.Q. 69th Brigade.	03/01/1917	03/01/1917
Heading	War Diary Of 9th Yorkshire Regiment. From December 1st To December 31st 1916 (Volume 17).		
War Diary	Ypres	01/12/1916	01/12/1916
War Diary	Trenches	03/12/1916	03/12/1916
War Diary	Ypres	07/12/1916	07/12/1916
War Diary	Trenches	11/12/1916	11/12/1916
War Diary	Divisional Reserve	15/12/1916	15/12/1916
War Diary	Zillebeke Bund	23/12/1916	23/12/1916
War Diary	Trenches	27/12/1916	27/12/1916
War Diary	Zillebeke Bund	31/12/1916	31/12/1916
Heading	War Diary Of 9th Yorkshire Regiment. From Jany 1st 1917 To Jany 31st 1917 (Volume 18).		
War Diary	Zillebeke Bund	01/01/1917	01/01/1917
War Diary	Trenches	04/01/1917	04/01/1917
War Diary	Divisional Reserve	08/01/1917	08/01/1917
War Diary	Trenches	16/01/1917	16/01/1917
War Diary	Ypres	20/01/1917	20/01/1917
War Diary	Trenches	24/01/1917	24/01/1917
War Diary	Ypres	28/01/1917	28/01/1917
Heading	War Diary Of 9th Yorkshire Regt. From 1st Feby 1917 To 28th Feby 1917 (Volume 19).		
War Diary	Ypres	01/02/1917	01/02/1917
War Diary	Divisional Reserve	01/02/1917	01/02/1917
War Diary	Kruisstraat	09/02/1917	09/02/1917
War Diary	Trenches	13/02/1917	13/02/1917
War Diary	Kruisstraat	17/02/1917	17/02/1917
War Diary	Trenches	21/02/1917	21/02/1917
War Diary	Montreal Camp	25/02/1917	25/02/1917
War Diary	Y Camp	27/02/1917	27/02/1917
War Diary	Bollezeele	28/02/1917	28/02/1917
Heading	War Diary Of 9th Yorkshire Regiment. From March 1st To March 31st (Volume 20).		
War Diary	Moulle	01/03/1917	01/03/1917
War Diary	Bollezeele	19/03/1917	19/03/1917
War Diary	Houtkerque	20/03/1917	30/03/1917
War Diary	P Camp	21/03/1917	21/03/1917
Heading	War Diary Of 9th Yorkshire Regiment. From April 1st 1917 To April 30th 1917 (Volume 21).		
War Diary	P Camp	01/04/1917	01/04/1917
War Diary	Montreal Camp	06/04/1917	06/04/1917
War Diary	Railway Dugouts	14/04/1917	14/04/1917
War Diary	Trenches	18/04/1917	18/04/1917
War Diary	Montreal Camp	22/04/1917	22/04/1917
War Diary	Zillebeke Bund	25/04/1917	25/04/1917
War Diary	Steenvoorde Area	29/04/1917	29/04/1917
War Diary	Poperinghe	29/04/1917	29/04/1917
War Diary	Steenvoorde Area	30/04/1917	30/04/1917
Miscellaneous	9th Yorkshire Regiment Operation Orders For Raid On Enemy Sap On Night Of 21/22 April 1917	21/04/1917	21/04/1917
War Diary	Steenvoorde Area	01/05/1917	01/05/1917
War Diary	Heksken	01/05/1917	01/05/1917

Type	Description	Start	End
War Diary	Montreal Camp	13/05/1917	13/05/1917
War Diary	Trenches	18/05/1917	18/05/1917
War Diary	Boeschepe Area	18/05/1917	18/05/1917
Miscellaneous	9th Yorkshire Regiment. Operation Orders For Raid On Hostile Trenches On Night Of 20/21st May 1917	20/05/1917	20/05/1917
Miscellaneous	9th Yorkshire Regiment. Report On Raid On Night Of 20/21st May 1917	20/05/1917	20/05/1917
War Diary	Boeschepe Area	01/06/1917	01/06/1917
War Diary	Scottish Lines And "N" Camp	01/06/1917	01/06/1917
War Diary	Railway Dugouts	05/06/1917	05/06/1917
War Diary	S.P.9	06/06/1917	06/06/1917
War Diary	Trenches	07/06/1917	07/06/1917
War Diary	Larch Wood Tunnels	09/06/1917	09/06/1917
War Diary	Vancouver Camp	11/06/1917	11/06/1917
War Diary	Berthen Area R. 31.d. 5.2	13/06/1917	13/06/1917
War Diary	Dickebusch H.28.d. 6.5	20/06/1917	20/06/1917
War Diary	Camp N2.c.5.4	24/06/1917	24/06/1917
War Diary	Camp H.33.c.3.6	27/06/1917	27/06/1917
War Diary	Dickebusch H.34.a.3.7	28/06/1917	28/06/1917
Miscellaneous	Appendix "A" Concentration Of Units From W To Z Day.		
Miscellaneous	X Scheme 69th Brigade Instruction No. 1	24/05/1917	24/05/1917
Miscellaneous	9th Yorkshire Regiment. Report On The Attack On Battle Wood On 7th June 1917	07/06/1917	07/06/1917
Map	Map No 1 Hill 60 Sector. Brigade H.Q. Battn H.Q.		
Map	Map. 2 1st Objective Red Battn Boundys Yellow.		
Miscellaneous	9th Yorkshire Regiment Appendix I.	02/07/1917	02/07/1917
Miscellaneous	9th Yorkshire Regiment. Appendix II.	02/07/1917	02/07/1917
Miscellaneous	O.C. 11th West Yorkshire Regt.	27/05/1917	27/05/1917
War Diary	Dickebush	01/07/1917	01/07/1917
War Diary	Steenvoorde Area	04/07/1917	04/07/1917
War Diary	Mic Mac Camp	11/07/1917	11/07/1917
War Diary	Hedge St Tunnels	11/07/1917	19/07/1917
War Diary	Mic Mac Camp	23/07/1917	23/07/1917
War Diary	Berthen Area	23/07/1917	23/07/1917
War Diary	La Wattine Quercamp West Becourt Bouvelinghem.	26/07/1917	26/07/1917
War Diary	Boisdinghem Zutove.	30/07/1917	30/07/1917
Miscellaneous	Appendix 9th Yorkshire Regiment		
Heading	9th Yorkshire Regt. War Diary Vol. 25 From August 1st 1917 To August 31st 1917. Vol 25		
War Diary	Boisdinghem Zutove	01/08/1917	09/08/1917
War Diary	Moulle	09/08/1917	09/08/1917
War Diary	Dallington Camp	24/08/1917	24/08/1917
War Diary	Dickebusch	25/08/1917	27/08/1917
Heading	War Diary Of 9th Yorkshire Regt From Sept 1st 1917 To Sept 30th 1917 (Volume 26).		
War Diary	Steenvoorde Area	02/09/1917	02/09/1917
War Diary	Lederzeele	03/09/1917	12/09/1917
War Diary	Steenvoorde Area	13/09/1917	13/09/1917
War Diary	Westoutre	14/09/1917	14/09/1917
War Diary	Micmac Area.	16/09/1917	16/09/1917
War Diary	Railway Dugouts	18/09/1917	24/09/1917
War Diary	Dickebusch Area	24/09/1917	24/09/1917
War Diary	Westoutre Area	25/09/1917	26/09/1917
War Diary	Stirling Castle	27/09/1917	30/09/1917

Heading	War Diary Of 9th Yorkshire Regt. From 1st Octr. 1917 To 31st Octr. 1917 (Volume 27).		
War Diary	Trenches	01/10/1917	01/10/1917
War Diary	Ridge Wood	02/10/1917	02/10/1917
War Diary	Berthen Area	03/10/1917	08/10/1917
War Diary	Wood Camp. S.	09/10/1917	09/10/1917
War Diary	No. 1 Area	10/10/1917	10/10/1917
War Diary	Bund	11/10/1917	11/10/1917
War Diary	Trenches	13/10/1917	16/10/1917
War Diary	No. 1. Area	18/10/1917	19/10/1917
War Diary	Boisdinghem	20/10/1917	31/10/1917
Miscellaneous	Appendix "A"	19/09/1917	19/09/1917
Miscellaneous	Appendix "B" Casualties During September 1917		

WO 95
2184/3.
9th Btn Yorks
1915 Aug - 1917 Oct

23RD DIVISION
69TH INFY BDE

9TH BN YORKSHIRE REGT.
AUG 1915 — ~~AUG 1916~~
1917 OCT

To Italy

Army Form C. 2118.

WAR DIARY
or
INTELLIGENCE SUMMARY.
(*Erase heading not required.*)

Instructions regarding War Diaries and Intelligence Summaries are contained in F. S. Regs., Part II and the Staff Manual respectively. Title pages will be prepared in manuscript.

Place	Date	Hour	Summary of Events and Information	Remarks and references to Appendices

2353 Wt. W2544/1454 700,000 5/15 D. D. & L. A.D.S.S./Forms/C. 2118.

121/6607

69 23rd Division

9th Yorkshire Regt.
Vol: I
Jun 23 – 31. 8. 15

Aug 15

I.A.
5 sheets

Army Form C. 2118.

WAR DIARY
INTELLIGENCE SUMMARY.
(Erase heading not required.)

Instructions regarding War Diaries and Intelligence Summaries are contained in F. S. Regs., Part II. and the Staff Manual respectively. Title pages will be prepared in manuscript.

Place	Date	Hour	Summary of Events and Information	Remarks and references to Appendices
BRAMSHOTT	23/8/15	6 pm.	Orders for departure received	
do	24/8/15			
do	25/8/15	11.20am	1st train consisting of Transport & advance party left LIPHOOK STATION for HAVRE. 30 officers 106 other ranks	
			72 horses 23 vehicles & B.Co.	
do	26/8/15	6.55pm	2nd train consisting of 150 horses 455 other ranks left LIPHOOK STATION for FOLKESTONE.	
do		7.35pm	3rd do do do 12 do 434 do do	
BOULOGNE	27/8/15	1.30am	Arrived BOULOGNE, & proceeded to OSTRAHOVE LARGE CAMP	
		2.30am	OSTRAHOVE LARGE CAMP.	
do		8.10pm	Marched to PONT AUX BRIQUES Railway Station.	
do		9.20pm	Arrived Station	
do		11.35pm	Entrained. 1 man left behind owing to illness	
WATTEN	28/8/15	3.45am	Arrived WATTEN STATION.	
		4.56am	Detrained	
		5.35am	Marched off	
MENTQUE NORTBECOURT		7.10am	Arrived	
		9.40am	do.	

Army Form C. 2118.

WAR DIARY
INTELLIGENCE SUMMARY.
(Erase heading not required.)

Place	Date	Hour	Summary of Events and Information	Remarks and references to Appendices
MENTQUE to NORTBECOURT	29/8/15 to 31/8/15		Remained in billets. Horse Powder issued owing to accid. out. 29/8/15	

Instructions regarding War Diaries and Intelligence Summaries are contained in F. S. Regs., Part II. and the Staff Manual respectively. Title pages will be prepared in manuscript.

121/7051

L.A.
5 sheets

23rd Division

9th Yorkshires
vol 2
Sept. 15

Confidential

War Diary
of
9th Yorks Regt

From 1st September to 30th September 1915 inclusive

Vol: 2

Army Form C. 2118.

WAR DIARY
—or—
INTELLIGENCE SUMMARY.
(Erase heading not required.)

Instructions regarding War Diaries and Intelligence Summaries are contained in F. S. Regs., Part II and the Staff Manual respectively. Title pages will be prepared in manuscript.

Place	Date	Hour	Summary of Events and Information	Remarks and references to Appendices
	1915			
NORBECOURT	Sept 1st to Sep 5th		In billets	
do	6th	5.30am	Left NORTBECOURT & marched to WALLONS SUR CHEEL arriving there 2.30pm. (breeze)	
			in neighbourhood.	
WALLONSSURCHEEL	7th	8.30am	Marched to VIEUX BERQUIN arriving 2.30pm. Billeted in neighbourhood.	
VIEUX BERQUIN	8th		In billets.	
do	9th	9.30am	Marched to RUE DELPIERRE arriving at 2.30pm. Billeted in neighbourhood.	
RUE DELPIERRE	10th		Instruction in trench & billets under 2nd Cameron Highlanders 1st Royal Scots.	
	11th			
	12th		Returned to VIEUX BERQUIN, billeted in neighbourhood	
VIEUX BERQUIN	13th			
do	14th		In billets.	
do	15th	11.15am	Marched RUE de BIEZ arriving 4pm.	
RUE de BIEZ	16th		In billets in reserve	
	17th		"C" Coy moved into 3rd line Trench on BOIS GRENIER fene.	
	18th		do	

Army Form C. 2118.

WAR DIARY
INTELLIGENCE SUMMARY.
(Erase heading not required.)

Instructions regarding War Diaries and Intelligence Summaries are contained in F. S. Regs., Part II. and the Staff Manual respectively. Title pages will be prepared in manuscript.

Place	Date	Hour	Summary of Events and Information	Remarks and references to Appendices
RO Fde BIEZ	1915 Sept 19th		Two Companies (C & D) shell in 3rd line trenches. Remaining Coys in billets.	Sgd
	20th		A Coy H.Q. moved to 3rd line	Sgd
	21st	9 am	Heavy bombardment by our Artillery all day, commencing 9 a.m. Very little reply from enemy.	Sgd
	22nd		Shell in trenches. B Coy moved up from billets.	Sgd
	23rd		Shell in trenches.	Sgd
	24th		Shell in reserve. Stood by ready to advance to trench 10th West Riding Regt in case of advance.	Sgd
	25th	4 am	Heavy bombardment by our artillery. Jer Sky reply.	Sgd
		4.30 am		
	26th		Shell in trenches	Sgd
	27th		Moved into LA BESÉE Section of Trenches relieved 8th Yorks Regt	Sgd
	28th		Shell in Trenches. Nothing of importance to write.	Sgd
	29th		1st Casualty. One man slightly wounded by Shrapnel.	Sgd
	30th		Nothing to record.	Sgd

121/7595

1a   S.A.
      4 sheets

23rd Kuraun

J. K. Yorkshire RSF.
Vol 3

Oct 15

Q

Confidential

War Diary

of

9th Yorks Regt.

From 1st October to 31st October 1915 Inclusive

Vol: 3

31/10/15 — Lt Chapman
Transport Officer 9th Yorks Regt

Army Form C. 2118.

WAR DIARY
or
INTELLIGENCE SUMMARY.
(Erase heading not required.)

Instructions regarding War Diaries and Intelligence Summaries are contained in F. S. Regs., Part II. and the Staff Manual respectively. Title pages will be prepared in manuscript.

Place	Date	Hour	Summary of Events and Information	Remarks and references to Appendices
BOIS GRENIER LINE	1.7.15		In trenches	Full.
L'HALLOBEAU	2.7.15	7.30p	Relieved by 12th D.L.I. & proceeded to L'HALLOBEAU. v. fine.	Full.
	3.7.15	8.30am	Marched to billets 1½ miles outside ESTAIRES.	Full.
ESTAIRES	4.7.15	5.30pm	" in town of ESTAIRES	Full.
"	4.7.15		In billets in ESTAIRES.	Full.
"	10.7.15		1st augt 15 officers & recruits left ESTAIRES — marched to billets at FORT ROMPU arriving 10 a.m.	Full.
"	8.7.15	7.45		Full.
FORT ROMPU	11.7.15	6 pm	Left FORT ROMPU & proceeded to billets in RUE MARLE.	Full.
RUE MARLE	11.7.15		In billets in RUE MARLE.	Full.
"	15.7.15	7.00p	Relieved 8th Yorks Regt in Trenches 59, 60, 61, & 62.	Full.
TRENCHES	16.7.15 to 19.7.15		In trenches. During the tour there were 8 casualties. 7 killed 1 wounded (all other ranks)	Full.
	20.7.15		Relieved by W. Yorks left in SS Rue of Trenches — also BOIS GRENIER line & Coy to billets in RUE MARLE	Full.
	20.7.15			Full.
	21.7.15 to 23.7.15		In trenches – During the tour there were 11 casualties - all wounded (all other ranks)	Full. Full. Full.
RUE MARLE	24.7.15	8 pm	Relieved by 9th York & Lanc Regt & proceeded to billets in RUE MARLE	Full.
do	24.7.15 to 31.7.15		In billets in RUE MARLE	Full.
do	30.7.15		2nd draft of 30 other ranks received.	Full.

33 *Strain*

9ᵗʰ Yorkshire
vol: 4

124 / 7/824

Nov 15.

Q

Confidential

WAR DIARY

OF
9th Yorks Regiment

From 1st to 30th November 1915
(Inclusive)

Volume 4

Norman Humphreys
Lt & Adjt for
Lt Col Comdg
9th Yorks Regt

30/11/15

Army Form C. 2118.

WAR DIARY
INTELLIGENCE SUMMARY.
(Erase heading not required.)

Place	Date	Hour	Summary of Events and Information	Remarks and references to Appendices
RUE MARLE	1 XI 15 to 5 XI 15		In billets. 13 men wounded by enemy shell in billets on 4. XI. 15	
T 59.60,61,62	6 XI 15	7.45 pm	Relieved 2nd Northants Regt in T 59.60.61.&62. Casualties 6 XI 15 – 10 XI 15 4 K 7 W	
do	10 XI 15	7.30 pm	Moved to BOIS GRENIER line in relief of 8th Yorks Regt. Weather v. cold.	
BOIS GRENIER LINE	18 XI 15	6.30 pm	Relieved by 11th West Yorks Regt. & proceeded to billets in RUE MARLE. v. cold v wet.	
RUE MARLE	21 XI 15	6.45 pm	Relieved 1st Sherwood Foresters in T 11th West Yorks in T 57.58.59.60 & 61. v wet.	
T 57 58 sq b0 b1	24 XI 15	6.40 pm	Relieved by 10th York & Lancs. & proceeded to billets at FORT ROMPU	
FORT ROMPU	25 XI 15 to 30 XI 15		In billets at FORT ROMPU. v wet. weather v cold.	

S. Norman Hunnybun
Lt A-p for
LtCol Comm'd
8th Yorks Regt

30/11/15

— Confidential —

9 Yorks Reg
Vol. 5

XXIII

WAR DIARY

OF

9th Yorkshire Regiment

From 1st Decr 1915 to 31st Decr 1915

(VOLUME V).

Certified true copy

2/1/16

(Sd) A. Hemmyhon Lieut Colonel
Commdg IX Yorkshire Regt

5 A.
2 shields

Certified Copy of Duplicate **WAR DIARY** for month of December 1916. Army Form C. 2118.
(Originals forwarded to the Officer i/c War
Diaries, Adjutant General's Office, at the Base on the 30/12/16)

INTELLIGENCE SUMMARY.

(Erase heading not required.)

Instructions regarding War Diaries and Intelligence
Summaries are contained in F. S. Regs. Part II.
and the Staff Manual respectively. Title pages
will be prepared in manuscript.

Place	Date	Hour	Summary of Events and Information	Remarks and references to Appendices
FORT ROMPU	1-6		In Billets	AA
RUE DELETTRE	6-10		do	AA
Trip. 48.49.50.51	10-14		In Trenches – returned in Billets Casualties 2 K 3 W.	AA
RUE DELETTRE	14-18		In Billets relieved by	AA
Trip. 48.49.50.51 18-22			In Trenches relieved do Casualties O.R. 1 W.	AA
L'HALLOBEAU	22-29		In Billets relieved by 1st D.L.I.	AA
Trip. 12.13.14.15.16 29-31			In Trenches – Casualties Officer 1 Wounded O.R. 1 Killed	AA

(Signed) G.H. Shuttleworth Lynch(?)
Lt. Colonel
Commanding 9th Yorks Regt.

Dec 27 IX York Regt.

Certified true copy.

[signature]
30/12/16

Lieut & Adjt for
Lt. Colonel
Commanding 9th Yorkshire Regt.

Confidential

War Diary
of
9th Yorkshire Regiment

From 1st January 1916 to 31st January 1916
(Inclusive)

Vol 6

Lt Col
1st Rgt
Yorkshire
21/1/16

Army Form C. 2118.

WAR DIARY
INTELLIGENCE SUMMARY.
(Erase heading not required.)

Instructions regarding War Diaries and Intelligence Summaries are contained in F. S. Regs., Part II. and the Staff Manual respectively. Title pages will be prepared in manuscript.

Place	Date	Hour	Summary of Events and Information	Remarks and references to Appendices
	1916 January			
I.16.1 to I.21.2	1st	12.25am	Successful raid carried out on German trenches commanded by Lieut. H.K. Pain & party of 8 piloted by Capt G.K. THOMPSON & a party of about 100 men. Casualties. 1 Officer died of wounds. 1 Officer wounded. OR 1 Killed 14 wounded.	full
RUE MARLE	2nd	6.20pm	To billets. Relieved by 10th WEST RIDING REGT	full
I.16.1 to I.21.2	6th		To trenches on relief of do. Casualties OR 3 wounded.	full
RUE MARLE	10th		To billets. Relieved by do.	full
RUE DORCHOIRE	11th		do. Taken over from 11th Northumberland Fusiliers.	full
I.31.1 to I.31.5	23rd		To trenches in relief of 1st WORCESTERSHIRE REGT. Casualties OR 2 Killed 4 wounded.	full
do	27th	10.25am to 10.40pm	Terrific bombardment of I.31.1 to I.31.4 Casualties 1 Officer wounded. OR 4 killed & about 9 wounded.	full
RUE DELETTREE	29th		To billets. Relieved by 11th West Yorks Regt.	full
I.31.1 to I.31.5	31st		To trenches on relief of do.	full

H.J.S Prior Major
Comdg 9th Yorks Regt.

31/1/16

SECRET.   First Army No.502/5 (G)
                                                d/- 10/1/16.

Summary of report on raid carried out in the early morning of
January 1st by the 9th Battalion Yorkshire Regt. of the 69th
Infantry Brigade, 23rd Division, in the neighbourhood of the
RUE DU BOIS.

The men who were to take part in the raid were struck off duty for
some days prior to the 1st January and were practised in every detail
on ground where trenches had been dug to represent the German works to
be attacked.

For several days previous to the attack the artillery cut the
enemy's wire and bombarded his parapet at various points along the front
of the 23rd Division, including the point at which the raid was to be
made.

It was noticed that the enemy was becoming more and more alert,
and at the risk of his wire not being completely cut, the artillery wire
cutting was stopped all along the front for two days prior to the night
fixed for the raid.

Details of the actual raid.
The attacking party was under the command of Major Prior.

The night of the 31st December - 1st January was still and starlight.
The enemy's trenches were about 250 yards from the point of exit from
our own trenches. The enemy was very much on the alert and was using,
in addition to numerous Very lights, three searchlights.

At 9-30 p.m. on the 31st December a wire cutting party, under the
command of 2nd Lieut. Armitage, 9th Yorkshire Regiment, crossed to the
enemy's lines and successfully cut a lane about 5 feet wide through the
enemy's wire. The wire cutting party was left at the wire and the
officers returned to our own trenches at 11-30 p.m. and reported that
the way was clear to the enemy's parapet and that there would be little
difficulty in crossing the borrow pit.

At 12-15 a.m. the raiding parties left our trenches and proceeded
to a place of assembly in front of our line. From here the parties
crawled very slowly towards the enemy position and on nearing it were
met by the wire cutting party who guided them to the lane which had been
cut.

It was necessary in order to ensure success that the raid and the
accompanying artillery support should be simultaneous. It had conse-
quently been arranged that the infantry attack and artillery should act
in accordance with a pre-arranged time table.

The artillery barrage started at 1-33 a.m. and at this moment the
enemy's trenches were successfully rushed by the raiding parties.

The parties, on entering the enemy's line, proceeded at once to
bomb to the right and left of the point of entry.

The Right Party, under 2nd Lieut. Gibson, found the enemy's trench
lightly held. The party accounted for four Germans who were either
bombed or bayonetted.

The Left Party, which was under the command of Capt. Thompson, was
attacked by the enemy with bombs, but the hostile bombers were driven
off. Fifteen Germans are reported to have been bayonetted by the party
and it is thought that probably five or ten more were killed exclusive
of others who took to flight and were driven into the artillery barrage.

About 35 of our men in all entered the enemy's trenches. This
number was found to be quite sufficient. The parties left the enemy's
trenches at 1-48 a.m. bringing their wounded (seven in all) with them.
No men were killed.
The enemy was undoubtedly surprised and only offered feeble resistance.
A password was used and this was found very useful.

9th Yorkshires
Vol 6

23rd

6.A.

CONFIDENTIAL

War Diary
of
9th Yorkshire Regt.

from 1st — 29th February 1916.

Vol. 7.

Returned to Officer i/c
War Diaries
Comm'dg 9th Yorks. Regt.

Army Form C. 2118.

Vo27

WAR DIARY
INTELLIGENCE SUMMARY.
(Erase heading not required.)

Instructions regarding War Diaries and Intelligence Summaries are contained in F. S. Regs. Part II and the Staff Manual respectively. Title pages will be prepared in manuscript.

Place	Date	Hour	Summary of Events and Information	Remarks and references to Appendices
	February			
T.31.1 to T.31.5.	1-4		In trenches. Casualties 10 Officer wounded. O.R. 2 Killed 5 wounded	Init
RUE DELETTRE	4		Moved to huts. Relieved by 1/1 K. WEST YORKS REGT. Casualties 30 Rwounded	Init
JESUS FARM.	8		do.	Init
VIEUX BERQUIN	14		Moved to A Billets.	Init
STEENBECQUE	15		" Camp.	Init
ESTAIRES	23		" Billets	Init
STEENBECQUE	27		Returned to Camp	Init

Normen Hepworth
Lt Col Comd
9th/Yorks Regt.

Confidential

War Diary
of
9th Yorkshire Regiment

from 1/3/16 to 31/3/16

Vol 8

Norman Hunnybun
Lt & A.A.
for Lt Colonel
9th Yorkshire Regt.

31/3/16

Army Form C. 2118.

WAR DIARY
INTELLIGENCE SUMMARY.
(Erase heading not required.)

Instructions regarding War Diaries and Intelligence
Summaries are contained in F. S. Regs., Part II.
and the Staff Manual respectively. Title pages
will be prepared in manuscript.

Place	Date	Hour	Summary of Events and Information	Remarks and references to Appendices
RUITZ	1/3/16 to 4/3/16		On billets	
GOUY SERVINS	4/3/16 to 6/3/16		do	
SOUCHEZ	6/3/16 8/3/16	3am 11pm	Relieved FRENCH in left subsector of SOUCHEZ sector. Casualties 2 OR wounded. Relieved by 10th WEST RIDING REGT moved to billets at VILLERS AU BOIS.	
VILLERS AU BOIS	10/3/16	9pm	Relieved 1st SHERWOOD FORESTERS in support trenches NOTRE DAME DE LORETTE.	
BOIS DE BOUVIGNY	14/3/16	9pm	Relieved by 1st LONDON REGT moved to huts at BOIS DE BOUVIGNY.	
CARENCY CHATELAIN	15/3/16		Moved to billets.	
			do	
FOSSE 10	19/3/16 25/3/16 30/3/16	11am 10am	Relieved 10 WEST RIDING REGT in left subsector of BULLY GRENAY NO 2. Casualties 2 OR wounded. Relieved by do moved to billets at FOSSE 10.	

[signature]
Lt.A/Adjt
1st Col Comdt
9th [York & Lancs Regt]
31/3/16

9 Yorks Reg vol 9

— CONFIDENTIAL —

XXIII

WAR DIARY

OF

9ᵀᴴ YORKSHIRE REGIMENT

FROM 1ˢᵀ APRIL 1916 TO 30ᵀᴴ APRIL 1916

VOLUME IX

9.A
2 sheets

Lieut & Adjt for
Lt Colonel
Commanding IX Yorkshire Regt

30/4/16

Army Form C. 2118.

VOL 9
WAR DIARY
or
INTELLIGENCE SUMMARY.
(Erase heading not required.)

Instructions regarding War Diaries and Intelligence Summaries are contained in F. S. Regs., Part II. and the Staff Manual respectively. Title pages will be prepared in manuscript.

Place	Date	Hour	Summary of Events and Information	Remarks and references to Appendices
	April			
FOSSE 10	1-4	In billets.		Appx
ANGRES	4-10	In trenches	Casualties OR 5 wounded.	Appx
FOSSE to HERSIN	10-16	In billets	do OR 4 " (1 since died of wounds)	Appx
HERSIN	16-18	do		Appx
CAMBLAIN CHATELAIN	18-19	do		Appx
FEBVIN PALFART	19-20	do		Appx
RECLINGHEM	20-25	do	Casualties 1 OR (accidentally admitted)	Appx
FEBVIN PALFART	25-26	do		Appx
HERSIN	26-30	do		Appx

Norman Hunnington
F. Ashton
Lt Col Comdg
1st Herts Regt.

YR34 Vol. 10 XXIII

10.A
2 sheets

Capt & Adjt. for
O.C. 9th Yorkshire Regt.

War Diary
of
9ᵗʰ Yorkshire Regt.

From 1-5-16 to 31-5-16

Volume 10

Army Form C. 2118.

WAR DIARY

~~INTELLIGENCE~~ SUMMARY.

(Erase heading not required.)

Instructions regarding War Diaries and Intelligence Summaries are contained in F. S. Regs., Part II. and the Staff Manual respectively. Title pages will be prepared in manuscript.

Place	Date	Hour	Summary of Events and Information	Remarks and references to Appendices
HERSIN	1/5/16		In billets. 1 O.R. wounded.	
OURTON	4/5/16		do.	
HERSIN	11/5/16		do.	
ANGRES 2	12/5/16		In trenches. Relieved 2 H.L.I. Casualties Killed 2 O.R. Died of wounds 2 O.R. wounded 9 O.R.	
BULLY GRENAY	17/5/16		In billets. Casualties. Killed 1 Officer. Died of wounds 1 Officer 1 O.R. wounded 1 O.R.	
ANGRES 2	22/5/16		In trenches. Casualties	
FOSSE 10 & BULLY GRENAY	26/5/16		In billets Casualties 1. O.R wounded	
VERDREL	30/5/16		In billets	

Norman Arrington
Capt & A/Adjt for O.C.
9th Yorks Regt.

9 Yorks Regt
Vol 11
June

11.A.
2 sheets

[signature]
Capt. & Adjt.
For O.C. 9th Yorks Regt.

CONFIDENTIAL XXIII

WAR DIARY
OF
9TH YORKSHIRE REGT.

FROM JUNE 1ST 1916 TO JUNE 30TH 1916

(VOLUME XI)

Army Form C. 2118.

WAR DIARY
INTELLIGENCE SUMMARY.
(Erase heading not required.)

Place	Date	Hour	Summary of Events and Information	Remarks and references to Appendices
VERDREL	1/6/16		In billets	
SOUCHEZ I	9/6/16		Relieved 11th Northumberland Fusiliers in trenches	
FOSSE 10	13/6/16		In billets - Relieved by 6th London Regiment	
PERNES	14/6/16		do.	
SERNY	15/6/16		1 O.R. accidentally wounded	
LONGUEAU	24/6/16		Entrained at BERGUETTE station for LONGUEAU & arrived there about 11am, 25.6.16	
ST SAUVEUR	25/6/16		The same night to billets at ST SAUVEUR.	

30/6/16

Sutherland
CAPT. & ADJT.
FOR O.C. 9TH YORKS REGT.

69th Inf.Bde.
23rd Div.

9th BATTN. THE YORKSHIRE REGIMENT.

J U L Y

1 9 1 6

20.
8/3

CONFIDENTIAL

WAR DIARY

OF

9TH YORKSHIRE REGT.

FROM JULY 1ST TO JULY 31ST 1916

(VOLUME 12)

W.H.Gamble 2/Lt a.adjt. for Major
Commanding 9th Yorkshire Regt.

Army Form C. 2118.

WAR DIARY
INTELLIGENCE SUMMARY.

(Erase heading not required.)

Instructions regarding War Diaries and Intelligence Summaries are contained in F. S. Regs., Part II. and the Staff Manual respectively. Title pages will be prepared in manuscript.

91.

Place	Date	Hour	Summary of Events and Information	Remarks and references to Appendices
ST. SAUVEUR	1-7-16		In billets	1074.
BAZIEUX	1-7-16		Bivouacs in wood	1044.
ALBERT	2-7-16		Bivouacs outside town	1046.
TRENCHES	3-7-16		Reserve trenches in evening. Front line system of trenches at night. H.Q. at CRAPES SPUR - Casualty:- 1 O.R. Died of Wounds.	1046.
DO	5-7-16		H.Q. moved to HELIGOLAND at 3 p.m. Battalion made an attack at 6 p.m. and captured HORSE-SHOE Trench. Casualties:- Officers:- 3 Killed, 4 Wounded, 2 reported Missing afterwards found to have been Killed in action. O.R. :- 14 Killed, 144 Wounded, 28 reported Missing. Prisoners captured during the advance 140, also 2 Machine Guns. Counter attacks by Germans on our left flank during night were unsuccessful	2016.
BELLE VUE FARM	6-7-16		Bivouacs, Relieved by 9th WELSH REGT - Casualties:- Officers 1 Killed.	1074.
DO	7-7-16		Stand to at 8 a.m in support for attack, but did not move off. Marched to Reserve trenches at 7.30 p.m in support for attack but returned to bivouacs about midnight. Heavy run.	1022.
Trenches	10-7-16		Left bivouacs at 11 a.m for trenches; arrived in assembly trench about 4 p.m (heavily shelled on way up) at 4.50 p.m the 8th & 9th Yorkshires left their assembly trenches to attack CONTALMAISON, the 8th YORKS being on the right, 9th YORKS on the left. We had to advance over the open for 1500 yards and lost heavily from Shrapnel, H.E. Machine Gun & rifle fire. Attack completely successful and CONTALMAISON was captured by 6 p.m and held. Over 250 prisoners were taken, many Germans killed, 8 Machine Guns captured, also large quantity of ammunition, but S.A.A. for Field Guns. Counter attacks by Germans were driven off. Casualties: Officers 3 Killed, 11 Wounded. O.R.:- 13 Killed, 192 Wounded, 24 reported missing.	1044.
BELLE VUE FARM	12-7-16		Bivouacs, Relieved by 1st BLACK WATCH REGT night of 11th / 12th	1044.

2333 Wt. W3144/1454 700,000 5/15 D.D.&L. A.D.S.S./Forms/C. 2118.

Army Form C. 2118.

WAR DIARY
or
INTELLIGENCE SUMMARY.
(Erase heading not required.)

Instructions regarding War Diaries and Intelligence Summaries are contained in F. S. Regs., Part II. and the Staff Manual respectively. Title pages will be prepared in manuscript.

Place	Date	Hour	Summary of Events and Information	Remarks and references to Appendices
FRANVILLERS	12·7·16		In billets	
MOLLIENS-AU-BOIS	13·7·16		In billets. 1 Officer wounded 10th inst died of wounds 14·7·16	
MILLENCOURT	21·7·16		In billets.	
Do.	23·7·16		Warned to be ready to move towards trenches at ½ hours notice after midnight, but were not required.	
ALBERT	26·7·16		In billets. Relieved 2nd K.R.R. Corps	
TRENCHES	28·7·16		Relieved 10th H.F. in reserve trenches at SCOTS REDOUBT. Casualties. 1 O.R. wounded.	
Do.	30·7·16		Relieved 10th WEST RIDING REGT. in front line system of trenches, O.G.1, O.G.2, MUNSTER ALLEY, GLOSTER ALLEY, X.5.d, X.6.c SHEET 57D S.E. 4.	
			Casualties; O.R. 1 Killed, 13 Wounded.	

15/8/16

W.H. Gambier 2/Lt. A/Adjt. for Major
Commanding 9th Yorkshire Regt.

37·
NB

69th Brigade.
23rd Division.

1/9th BATTALION

YORKSHIRE REGIMENT

AUGUST 1 9 1 6

9 Yorks Reg
Vol. 13

CONFIDENTIAL 29/69

WAR DIARY

OF

9ᵀᴴ YORKSHIRE REGT.

FROM AUGUST 1ˢᵀ 1916 TO AUGUST 31ˢᵀ 1916.

(VOLUME 13)

Army Form C. 2118.

WAR DIARY
or
INTELLIGENCE SUMMARY.
(Erase heading not required.)

Instructions regarding War Diaries and Intelligence Summaries are contained in F. S. Regs., Part II. and the Staff Manual respectively. Title pages will be prepared in manuscript.

Place	Date	Hour	Summary of Events and Information	Remarks and references to Appendices
Trenches	1-8-16		Front line system of Trenches (SOMME) Casualties: Wounded 1 Officer + 4 O.R.	A.R. Gardin
Do	2-8-16		Relieved by 13th D.L.I. and moved back to reserve trenches, PEAKE WOOD. Casualties O.R. 2 Killed, 11 Wounded.	WR&
Do	5-8-16		Relieved by 10th W. Riding Regt & moved to reserve trenches, SCOTS REDOUBT. Casualties O.R. 1 Wounded, 1 Missing.	WR&
Do	7-8-16		3 Companies relieved 8th Yorkshire Regt in front line system of trenches. 4th Company and H.Q. remained at SCOTS REDOUBT. Casualties: O.R. 4 Killed, 4 Wounded.	WR&
BRESLE	8-8-16		Billets. One company and Head Quarters at SCOTS REDOUBT relieved by 6th Cameron Highlander. 3 Companies in front line relieved by the King's Own Scottish Borderers.	WR&
YAUCOURT BUSSUS	11-8-16		Billets. Entrained at MERICOURT Station for PONT REMY and marched to YAUCOURT BUSSUS.	WR&
IN TRAIN	13-8-16		Entrained at PONT REMY Station for BAILLEUL	WR&
SCHAEKEN (in BERTHEN)	14-8-16		Billets. Detrained at BAILLEUL Station at 3 a.m. and marched to SCHAEKEN.	WR&
STEENWERCK	17-8-16		Billets.	WR&
PAPOT	18-8-16		Huts/tents. Relieved 21st K.R.R.	WR&
SOYER FARM	22-8-16		Reserve Billets. Relieved 8th Yorkshire Regt. Casualties: 1 O.R. Killed	WR&
GRESLOW FARM	25-8-16		Reserve Trenches. Relieved 11th D. Yorks Regt. Casualties 1 Officer Wounded	WR&
Do	31-8-16		Two small raids attempted on enemy's trenches at 11:30 p.m. Gas was liberated. Casualties Nil.	WR&

9th Yorkshire Regt
War Diary.
Sept. 1916

VOL 14

23/64

CONFIDENTIAL

WAR DIARY
OF
9TH YORKSHIRE REGT.

From Sept. 1st to Sept. 30th 1916.

(Volume 14)

1-10-16

35.
8/8

[signature] Lt a/adjt for
O.C. 9th Yorkshire Regt.

WAR DIARY
INTELLIGENCE SUMMARY.

Army Form C. 2118.

Place	Date	Hour	Summary of Events and Information	Remarks and references to Appendices
CRESLOW FARM PLOEGSTEERT	1-9-16		Reserve Trenches	A104
TRENCHES	2-9-16		Front Line System. Relieved 8th Yorkshire Regt. Casualties O.R. 1 Killed, 2 Wounded.	A104
Camp	4-9-16		Camp. Relieved by 7th East Lancs in Trenches and moved to 2nd A.N.Z.A.C. Training Camp.	A104
MOULLE	6-9-16		Billets. Entrained at BAILLEUL Station and detrained at ST. OMER, marched to MOULLE.	A104
COISY	11-9-16		Part Billets & part Bivouacs. Entrained at ST. OMER Station at midnight 10th-9-16 and detrained at LONGEAU, marched to COISY.	A104
HENENCOURT	12-9-16		Huts & Camons.	A104
MILLENCOURT	15-9-16		Part billets, & part bivouacs.	A105
TRENCHES	18-9-16		Front line System. Relieved 8th Seaforth Highlanders. Casualties Officers 1 Died of Wounds, 4 Wounded. O.R. 29 Killed, 15 Missing, 94 Wounded.	A104
Do.	21-9-16		2 Coys relieved by 2 Coys 8th Yorks Regt, & moved to reserve trench.	A104
Div. Reserve	22-9-16		Camp near ROUND WOOD. Relieved in trenches by 10th & 11th Northumberland Fusiliers. Casualties O.R. 3 accidentally wounded	A104
Brigade Reserve	26-9-16		Dugouts in the CUTTING near CONTALMAISON. Relieved 11th Batt. Notts & Derbys.	A104

36-EB

CONFIDENTIAL

WAR DIARY

OF

9TH YORKSHIRE REGT.

FROM OCT. 1ST 1916 TO OCT. 31ST 1916

(VOLUME 15)

1-11-16

[signature] Lt a/Adjutant for
O.C. 9th Yorkshire Regt.

Army Form C. 2118.

WAR DIARY
INTELLIGENCE SUMMARY
(Erase heading not required.)

Place	Date	Hour	Summary of Events and Information	Remarks and references to Appendices
TRENCHES	1-10-16		Reserve Trenches near MARTINPUICH Casualties, O.R. Killed 7, Wounded 18.	10726
Do.	5-10-16		Front Line System. Relieved 8th Yorkshire Regt. Casualties, O.R. Wounded 5	10726
Do	7-10-16		Battalion took part in attack on LE SARS, which was entirely successful. Casualties, Officers killed 2, Wounded 3.- O.R. killed 15, Wounded 86, Missing 10.	10726
CAMP	9-10-16		Relieved in trenches by Seaforth Highlanders (45th Brigade) and moved back to Camp near ROUND WOOD in early morning.	10726
ALBERT	9-10-16		Billets. Relieved in Camp by Cameron Highlanders (46th Brigade) and moved to billets in ALBERT.	10726
ENTRAINING	12-10-16		Entrained at ALBERT for LONGPRE	10726
CONTEVILLE	13-10-16		Detrained at LONGPRE about 8 p.m. and proceeded to CONTEVILLE by Motor bus. In Billets.	10726
POPERINGHE	15-10-16		Billets. Entrained at CONTEVILLE. Detrained at HOPOUTRE and marched to POPERINGHE	10726
YPRES	23-10-16		Billets in Hospice. Entrained at POPERINGHE. Detrained at YPRES. Relieved 12th D.L.I.	10726
Do.	26-10-16		Billets in INFANTRY BARRACKS. Changed billets from HOSPICE to BARRACKS.	10726
TRENCHES	29-10-16		Front line System and Support Trenches. Relieved 8th Yorkshire Regt.	10726

WAR DIARY or INTELLIGENCE SUMMARY

9th Yorkshire Regt. Vol 16

Army Form C. 2118.

Place	Date	Hour	Summary of Events and Information	Remarks and references to Appendices
TRENCHES	1-11-16		Left Sector, Front & Support Lines - Casualties 2 O.R. wounded	
DIVISIONAL RESERVE	4-11-16		Huts at Montreal Camp. Relieved in Trenches by 11th Sherwood Foresters	
YPRES	10-11-16		Billets in the Hospice. Relieved 11th Northumberland Fusiliers - Casualties O.R. 2 killed, 1 wounded	
TRENCHES	16-11-16		Right Sector, Front & Support Lines. Relieved 8th Yorkshire Regt. - Casualties O.R. 6 wounded	
DIVISIONAL RESERVE	22-11-16		Huts at Montreal Camp. Relieved in Trenches by 9th Yorks & Lancs. Regt.	
YPRES	29-11-16		Billets in the Barracks. Relieved 12th Durham Light Infantry.	

H.Q.
69th Brigade

Herewith original War Diary for
December 1916.

Please acknowledge receipt hereon.

3-1-17

W.W.Gamble Lt a/Adjt for
O.C. 9th Yorkshire Regt.

CONFIDENTIAL

WAR DIARY
OF
9TH YORKSHIRE REGIMENT.

FROM DECEMBER 1ST TO DECEMBER 31ST 1916.

(VOLUME 17)

Vol 17

W.R.9

Willcomb Lt a/adjt for
O.C. 9th Yorkshire Regt

Army Form C. 2118.

WAR DIARY
INTELLIGENCE SUMMARY
(Erase heading not required.)

Instructions regarding War Diaries and Intelligence Summaries are contained in F. S. Regs. Part II. and the Staff Manual respectively. Title pages will be prepared in manuscript.

Place	Date	Hour	Summary of Events and Information	Remarks and references to Appendices
YPRES	1-12-16		Billets in Barracks	
TRENCHES	3-12-16		Left Sector. Front & Support lines. Relieved 8th Yorkshire Regt.	
YPRES	7-12-16		Billets in Barracks. Relieved in trenches by 8th Yorkshire Regt.	
TRENCHES	11-12-16		Left Sector. Front & Support lines. Relieved 8th Yorkshire Regt.	
DIVISIONAL RESERVE	15-12-16		Huts at Montreal Camp. Relieved by 11th Sherwood Foresters in trenches.	
ZILLEBEKE BUND	23-12-16		Dugouts. Relieved 12" Durham Light Infantry.	
TRENCHES	27-12-16		Right Sector. Front & Support lines. Relieved 8th Yorkshire Regt.	
ZILLEBEKE BUND	31-12-16		Dugouts. Relieved in trenches by 8th Yorkshire Regt. – Casualties 1 O.R. Wounded.	

CONFIDENTIAL

WAR DIARY

of

9TH YORKSHIRE REGIMENT

From Jany 1st 1917
To Jany 31st 1917

(VOLUME 18)

Vol 18

Edward E. Appleyard
Lieut A/Adjt
9th Yorks Regt.

Army Form C. 2118.

WAR DIARY
INTELLIGENCE SUMMARY.
(Erase heading not required.)

Place	Date	Hour	Summary of Events and Information	Remarks and references to Appendices
ZILLEBEKE BUND	1-1-17		Dug-outs	92A
TRENCHES	4-1-17		Right Sector. Front & Support Lines. Relieved 8th Yorkshire Regt. Casualties 2 O.R. Wounded.	92A
DIVISIONAL RESERVE	8-1-17		Huts at MONTREAL CAMP. Relieved by 8th Yorks & Lancs Regt.	92A
TRENCHES	16-1-17		Left Sector. Front & Support Lines. Relieved 13th Durham Light Infantry. Casualties 1 O.R. Wounded.	92A
YPRES	20-1-17		Billets in BARRACKS. Relieved in trenches by 8th Yorkshire Regt. Casualties 2 O.R. Wounded.	92A
TRENCHES	24-1-17		Left Sector. Front & Support Lines. Relieved 8th Yorkshire Regt. Casualties 2 O.R. Killed 6 Wounded.	92A
YPRES	28-1-17		Billets in BARRACKS. Relieved in trenches by 8th Yorkshire Regt.	92A

CONFIDENTIAL.

WAR DIARY
of
9TH YORKSHIRE REGT.

From 1st Feby 1917 To 28th Feby 1917

(Volume 19)

95/19

Edward R. Appleyard
Lieut A/Adjutant
O.C. 9th Yorkshire Regiment

Army Form C. 2118.

WAR DIARY
or
INTELLIGENCE SUMMARY
(Erase heading not required.)

Instructions regarding War Diaries and Intelligence Summaries are contained in F. S. Regs., Part II. and the Staff Manual respectively. Title pages will be prepared in manuscript.

Place	Date	Hour	Summary of Events and Information	Remarks and references to Appendices
YPRES	1-2-17		Billets in Barracks. Moved to Montreal Camp. Relieved by 8th Yorks & Lancs.	99A
DIVISIONAL RESERVE	1-2-17		Units at Montreal Camp. Relieved by 12th D.L.I. Casualties 1 O.R. Died of Wounds.	99A
KRUISSTRAAT	9-2-17		One Company at KRUISSTRAAT, one at CAVALRY BARRACKS, one at BUND, one attached to 8th Yorks Regiment in Front Line. Relieved by 8th Yorks Regt. Casualties O.R. 5 Wounded.	99A
TRENCHES	13-2-17		Right Sector, 3 Coys in Front Line, "B" Coy at Brigade School. Relieved by 8th Yorkshire Regiment in Trenches Casualties O.R. 4 Wounded, 3 Killed.	99A
KRUISSTRAAT	17-2-17		One Coy at KRUISSTRAAT, 2 at BUND, one at CAVALRY BARRACKS Relieved by 8th Yorkshire Regiment	99A
TRENCHES	21-2-17		Right Sector, Front and Support Lines. Relieved in trenches by 13th Royal Sussex Regt. 39th Division. Casualties Officer Lt. H.G.Scott Wounded. O.R.3 Killed. 4 Wounded.	99A
MONTREAL CAMP	25-2-17		Huts.	99A
"Y" CAMP.	27-2-17		Moved to camp near HOUTKERQUE.	99A
BOLLEZEELE	28-2-17		Moved to billets.	99A

CONFIDENTIAL

WAR DIARY

OF

9TH YORKSHIRE REGT.

FROM MARCH 1ST TO MARCH 31ST
(VOLUME 20.)

Edward G. Appleyard
Lieut A/Adjt
9th Yorkshire Regt.

4-4-17.

Army Form C. 2118.

WAR DIARY
or
INTELLIGENCE SUMMARY.

(Erase heading not required.)

Instructions regarding War Diaries and Intelligence Summaries are contained in F. S. Regs., Part II. and the Staff Manual respectively. Title pages will be prepared in manuscript.

Place	Date	Hour	Summary of Events and Information	Remarks and references to Appendices
MOULLE	1-3-17		Moved to Billets in Army Reserve for Training	89A
BOLLEZEELE	19-3-17		Moved to Billets	89A
HOUTKERQUE	20-3-17		Moved to Billets	89A
"P" CAMP	21-3-17		Moved to Camp in PROVEN Area.	89A

CONFIDENTIAL

Vol 21

WAR DIARY
of
9TH YORKSHIRE REGIMENT.

From April 1st 1917.
To April 30th 1917.
(Volume 21)

Edward E. Appleyard
Lieut for Capt & Adjt
9th Bn Yorkshire Regt

2/5/17

Army Form C. 2118.

WAR DIARY
or
INTELLIGENCE SUMMARY.
(Erase heading not required.)

Place	Date	Hour	Summary of Events and Information	Remarks and references to Appendices
P Camp	1.4.17		Camp in PROVEN AREA	89A
Montreal Camp	6.4.17		Moor to Camp into Divisional Reserve. Relieved by 5th York & Lancs. Casualties 1 OR wounded 2 OR missing.	89A
Railway Dugouts	14.4.17		Here to Dugouts in Brigade Reserve. Three Coy's at Bund, one in RAILWAY DUGOUTS. Casualties 1 OR wounded. Relieved by 8th Yorks	89A
Trenches	16.4.17		Left Sector of Right Brigade. Two Coys in front line ST PETERS STREET — to GAP. One Coy in HALIFAX STREET, one Coy in MAPLE STREET. Suffered enemy gas at I 30 c 2.8½ found to be a loop line from the German front line on the night of 19/20. Small Raid planned for the night of 21/22 but raid was not successful owing to the Bangalore Torpedo failing to explode. Casualties 1 OR killed 1 OR died of wounds 14 OR wounded. Relieved by 5th York & Lancs.	89A
Montreal Camp	22.4.17		Here to Camp into Divisional Reserve	89A
Zillebeke Bund	25.4.17		"B" & "D" Coys hence to dugouts to supply working parties for Right sector of Divisional front	89A
Steenvoorde Area	29.4.17		Here to Billets into Corps Reserve at 15 hours notice.	89A
Poperinghe	29.4.17		"B" & "D" Coys here to billets	89A
Steenvoorde Area	30.4.17		"B" & "D" Coys here to billets into Corps Reserve.	89A

SECRET.
Map ZILLEBEKE
28 NW.4.& NE.3 (parts of)   9TH YORKSHIRE REGIMENT.
1/10,000

Copy No,...

OPERATION ORDERS
FOR
RAID ON ENEMY SAP ON NIGHT OF 21/22 APRIL 1917.

1. **OBJECT OF RAID.**
    To destroy Enemy Sap at I.30.c.2.8½.

2. **TIME OF RAID.**
    2 a.m. on morning of 22nd April 1917.

3. 2/Lt. M.G.Robson ("C" Coy) will be in command of raiding party which will consist of 2 parties of 1 N.C.O. and 6 O.R. wearing white bands on their arms, each composed as follows :-
    1 N.C.O. in charge.
    2 Bayonet Men.
    1 Bomber.
    1 Carrier.
    2 Fatigue men for carrying explosives, shovels etc.
    These parties will be formed up in our front line by 1.40 a.m.

4. Directly the Bangalore Torpedoe is exploded under the hostile wire, the above parties headed by the bayonet men will rush the enemy sap and work up his trench for about 30 yards, one party to the right and the other to the left, until a spot is reached where the charges can be exploded. They will then at once draw to a safe distance. As soon as the charges have been exploded a block will be made at the head of the trench communicating with our front line. This trench will be dug as quickly as possible by a party detailed by Capt W.F.Greenwood for that purpose. They will commence work directly the raiding party has left our trenches.

5. 2 Covering parties consisting of 1 N.C.O. and 3 Bombers will proceed to points outside the enemy sap on right and left, and will be outside the hostile wire in order to bomb any of the enemy moving down the trench to the assistance of their party in the sap. These covering parties should proceed with the greatest caution and should be in position by 1.45 am.

6. O.C. "C" Coy will arrange for the supply of all necessary material, including bombs, wire etc., required for the raid and will make all preparations for repelling counter attack.

7. All men in front line will stand to at 1.55 a.m. and will not stand down until ordered.

21/4/17.

(sd) E.E.APPLEYARD. Lieut. A/Adjt.
9th Yorkshire Regiment.

Copy No.1. 69th Infantry Brigade.
    2. Commanding Officer, 9th Yorks.R.
    3. 2/Lt. M.G.Robson.
    4. O.C. "A" Coy.
    5. O.C. "B" Coy.
    6. O.C. "C" Coy.
    7. O.C. "D" Coy.
    8. File.

Army Form C. 2118.

WAR DIARY
or
INTELLIGENCE SUMMARY.
(Erase heading not required.)

9 Yorkshire Regt Vol 22

Place	Date	Hour	Summary of Events and Information	Remarks and references to Appendices
STEENVOORDE AREA	1.5.17		In Billets for training in Corps Reserve.	
HENCKEN	1.5.17		Moved under canvas. Battalion employed on working parties.	
MONTREAL CAMP	13.5.17		Moved to Montreal Camp into Divisional Reserve.	
TRENCHES	18.5.17		Relieve 11th Northumberland Fusiliers in the Left Sector of the Right Brigade Front. Two Companies in the front line ST PETERS STREET – THE GAP. One Company in HALIFAX STREET. One Company in MAPLE STREET. Small raid carried out on the night of 20/21. A copy of operation orders & report on raid is attached. Casualties 4 OR killed 13 OR wounded. Relieved by 9th York & Lancs Regt on the night of 24th/25th & moved to BRANDHOEK & return for AREELE.	
BOESCHEPE AREA			Move to Billets in BOESCHEPE AREA into Divisional Reserve for training over model trenches for forthcoming offensive of 2nd Army.	

9TH YORKSHIRE REGIMENT.

OPERATION ORDERS FOR RAID ON HOSTILE TRENCHES ON NIGHT OF 20/21st MAY 1917.

No. 10.

Time. Zero will be 1 a.m. on 21st inst. at which hour the Raiding Parties will enter the hostile trenches through gaps already cut in the hostile wire opposite CANADA STREET about I.30.a.6.1.

Objects.
(1) To obtain information and Identification from prisoners.
(2) To counteract the present German policy of entering our lines periodically.

Objective. Hostile front line trenches about 50 yards on either side of I.30.a.6.1.

Detail of Parties. No.1.Party. 2/Lt.M.G.Robson and 16.O.R. to work to the Right for about 50 yards.
No.2.Party. 2/Lt.N.Groom and 10.O.R. to work to the Left for about 50 yards.
These parties will be sub-divided in accordance with the work already allotted to them. They will vacate the hostile line not later than 1.15 a.m.
2/Lt.M.G.Robson will be in command of the Raid.
2/Lt.R.L.Christie is responsible for the supply of all necessaries connected therewith, and the Bn.L.G.O. for the action of the Lewis Guns.
The above parties will be formed up at convenient places in the front line under their respective leaders not later than 12.15 a.m. All Identifications will be removed before forming up.

Artillery. No previous preparation, but a Box Barrage will open as detailed below at Zero plus 3, and will be intense until plus 15, then a slow rate of fire until ordered to cease by the Artillery F.O.O.-
TRENCH MORTARS. Will fire on hostile trenches round about I.30.c.3.2.
STOKES GUNS. On neighbourhood of crater and trench round it at at I.30.c.5.8. also on Trench Junction I.30.c.7.8.
MACHINE GUNS. To fire as available on area South, South East, and South West of MT. SORREL.
LEWIS GUNS. Will fire occasional bursts on selected points on hostile line both during and after the raid.
Trench Mortars, Stokes Guns, and Machine Guns will open fire at Zero and cease at 1.15 a.m. unless otherwise ordered.

Our Trenches. O.C. "B" Coy will be responsible for removing all obstacles that may impede free passage from his front line trenches, and for keeping a clear passage through them during the raid.
He will withdraw the garrison of the Post on the extreme Right from 12.50 a.m. to 1.30 a.m.

Synchronisation. 2/Lt.M.G.Robson and 2/Lt.N.Groom will report to Bn.H.Q. at 9 p.m. tonight for the purpose of synchronising watches with the Artillery Liason Officer.

Bn.H.Qrs. Advance Bn.Headquarters in CANADA STREET at "B"Coys H.Q.dugout from 12.30 a.m. until the close of operations.

Lieut.Colonel,
Commanding 9th Yorkshire Regiment.

No.1. 69th Inf.Bde.
2. " " (for C.R.A)
3. O.C. 9th Yorks Regt.
4. O.C. "B" Coy. 9th Yorks.
5. 2/Lt.M.G.Robson.
6. " N.Groom.
7. " R.L.Christie.
8. O.C.T.M.B.
9. L.G.O.
10. War Diary.

SECRET.   9TH YORKSHIRE REGIMENT.

REPORT ON RAID ON NIGHT OF 20/21st MAY 1917.

Detail of Parties.
No.1.Party. 2/Lt.M.G.Robson and 12.O.R.
No.2.Party. 2/Lt.N.Groom and 16.O.R.
Officer in command of attack 2/Lt.M.G.Robson.

At 12.50 a.m. both parties were in position 15 yards from enemy trench. At 1 a.m. the signal to rush was given by the officer in charge of the attack.

No.1.Party. The Officer and Bayonet men found no difficulty in entering the enemy's trench and at once moved to the right expecting to be followed by the rest of the party. There was no enemy to be seen but on moving along about 30 yards, a communication trench was found, and as the remainder of the party had not followed it was deemed inadvisable to proceed further.
On returning to the point of entry 3 more men jumped into the trench. Our Artillery had opened fire and several shells were falling short into the enemy wire. The enemy had also opened a very hot fire with rifle grenades.
The party proceeded along the trench again but came to a standstill close to the communication trench before-mentioned. The Officer thereupon jumped up on the parapet and threw a bomb, and the enemy replied with a hail of rifle grenades and bombs. A bomb carrier was wounded and had to leave the trench. The officer and one man then proceeded along the top but owing to our Artillery again firing short found it impossible to proceed, and as it was now 1.12 a.m. the officer decided to evacuate the trench and informed No.2.Party of his intention.

No.2.Party. The Officer and 3 men of No.2.Party entered the hostile trench simultaneously with the leading men of No.1. The advance proceeded down the trench to the left. Two of them were hit immediately, presumably by rifle grenades which were falling all round. The Officer and Bayonet man proceeded down the trench for about 30 yards when they saw one of the enemy about to fire a Very light. The Officer fired at him and he immediately ran away pursued by the Bayonet man for a short way. The Officer then decided to return and guard the rear of No.1.Party.

All our men left the hostile trench by 1.14 a.m. and returned without loss. 5 men had been wounded.
It has not yet been definately ascertained why the remainder of the party did not enter the trench but apparently they were caught in the hostile wire and were very much troubled by rifle grenades and shells falling short.

The enemy does not seem to occupy his front trench at night, but merely patrols it for the purpose of firing Very Lights. The rifle grenades and Egg bombs which were thrown by the enemy appeared to come from somewhere directly in rear of his front line. Absolutely no hostile Machine Gun fire was noticed during the raid, and there was no retaliation except from rifle grenades and a few T.M.Bombs.

Enemy Trench. This is a deep one in first class condition and has not been damaged by our Artillery. The floor is dry and boarded and the Rivetting consists of brushwork. There were no traverses in the trench at the point of entering which was absolutely straight for about 40 yards.

21/5/17.
                                              Lieut.Colonel.
                                    Commanding 9th Yorkshire Regiment.

Army Form C. 2118.

WAR DIARY
or
INTELLIGENCE SUMMARY.
(Erase heading not required.)

9 Yorkshire
Vol 23

Place	Date	Hour	Summary of Events and Information	Remarks and references to Appendices
BOESCHEPE AREA	1.6.17		In billets in Divisional Reserve training for 2nd Army Offensive. Perfect weather.	
SCOTTISH LINES AND "N" CAMP	1.6.17		Under canvas. Perfect weather.	
RAILWAY DUGOUTS	5.6.17		Moved to trenches. Perfect weather.	
S P 9	6.6.17		Moved to trenches preparatory to attack next morning — For disposition of Bn. and details of attack vide item "A" of Appendix I. Perfect weather.	A & I
TRENCHES	7.6.17	6.50 a.m	Attack on BATTLE WOOD — vide Copy report of C.O. (item "B" of Appendix I.) Perfect weather. Casualties vide Appendix II.	App I
LARCH WOOD TUNNELS	9.6.17		Relieved by 10th West Riding Regt. in the front line and moved into Brigade Reserve. Perfect weather.	Casualties as per Appendix II
VANCOUVER CAMP	11.6.17		In huts. Perfect weather.	
BERTHEN AREA R.31.d.5.2	13.6.17		In camp and billets for Divisional Rest and Re-organisation. Perfect weather.	
DICKEBUSCH H.28.d.6.5	20.6.17		Moved to camp to be employed on road making c.6.15 bays 8th Yorkshire Regt attached for same purpose. Perfect weather.	
CAMP N.2.c.5.H	24.6.17		Shelled out of camp at DICKEBUSCH and moved to Camp at N.2.c.5.H. Working parties on roads continued. Relieved by 15th Durh.	
CAMP H.33.c.3.6	27.6.17		Regt. and moved to camp H.33.c.3.6. Perfect weather. In Brigade Reserve to 70th Brigade. Bn moved same night to TRIANGULAR SPOIL BANK. Perfect weather.	
DICKEBUSCH H.34.a.3.7	28.6.17		In Brigade Reserve to 64th Brigade. Bn at TRIANGULAR SPOIL BANK relieved by 11th West Yorks Regt. Weather changed. Heavy thunderstorms and rain.	

APPENDIX "A".

CONCENTRATION OF UNITS FROM W TO Z DAY.

UNIT.	W DAY.	W/X NIGHT.	X/Y NIGHT.	Y/Z NIGHT.	REMARKS.
"A" Battalion. 10th West Riding Regt.	MONTREAL CAMP.	To RAILWAY DUGOUTS.	To Line. (Vide Map No.1)	—	
"B" Battalion. 8th Yorkshire Regt.	SCOTTISH LINES.	No Change.	To S.P.9. ("D" Bn. Area).	To Line. (Vide Map No.1).	Route. DEN GROENEN - KRUISSTRAAT - Bridge 14.
"C" Battalion. 11th West Yorkshire Regt.	Camp M.	To ZILLEBEKE BUND.	To Line. (Vide Map No.1).	—	
"D" Battalion. 9th Yorkshire Regt.	Camp N.	No Change.	To RAILWAY DUGOUTS.	To Right Support S.P.9. (Vide Map No.1)	Route via ZILLEBEKE.
"E" Battalion. 12th Durham L.Inf.	Line.	To YPRES.	No Change.	To Left Support (Vide Map No.1)	
"F" Battalion. 11th North'd.Fus.	RAILWAY DUGOUTS.	To Camp M.	No Change.	To Bde. Reserve.	
69th M.Gun Coy.	Camp.	No Change.	RAILWAY DUGOUTS	To Line.	Route as for "A" to "D" Battns.
69th T.M.Battery.	Camp.	No Change.	RAILWAY DUGOUTS	To Line.	

SECRET.   A   Copy No...3...

X SCHEME *=* 69TH BRIGADE INSTRUCTIONS NO.1.

Reference ZILLEBEKE Map 1/10,000
and Special Maps attached.

1. Objectives, dividing lines between Units and the position for assembly of Units are shewn on attached maps which are not to be reproduced.

2. In accordance with Divisional Instructions no papers dealing with the Scheme are to be kept in front of Brigade H.Q. when in the line.
   Officers, N.C.O's and men are strictly forbidden to enter into any conversation on the subject in public places or at any time except when required by duty.

3. The attack on HILL 60 Sub-Sector will be made by 69th Brigade plus two Battalions 68th Brigade.
   The 70th Brigade will attack MOUNT SORREL on the left of 69th Brigade, the inner flanks converging so as to meet at I.30.c.1.1.
   The 142nd Brigade of the 47th Division will attack on the Right of 69th Brigade.

4. There will be five days preliminary bombardment. Wire cutting on front and support trenches is now being continued daily. Gaps must be identified and kept under fire at night continuously. Where necessary gaps in our wire will be cut by hand on Y/Z night under orders of Battalion Commander.

5. The moves of Battalions prior to operations are shewn in Appendix "A".

6. The mines will be fired at Zero.
   A mine which does not explode within 15 seconds will not explode at all.
   The explosion of the mines will be the signal for the Artillery barrage to commence.

7. The Artillery barrage for the 47th Division and 69th Brigade with the exception of a few local differences on the left will be as follows :-

   (a). Barrage lifts off enemy's front line at Zero plus 3 minutes.
   (b). Barrage lifts off Red Line at Zero plus 20 and will pause at 200 yards till Zero plus 35 when it will again move forward.
   (c). Barrage lifts off Blue Line at Zero plus 45 for 200 yards where it will continue till Zero plus 3 hours 40 minutes when advance to Black Line will begin.
   (d). Barrage lifts off junction of OAF LANE and VERBRANDEN Road at Zero plus 4 hours for 200 yards and will pause till zero plus 4 hours 15 minutes when it will again move forward.

   In addition to the above heavy guns and howitzers will continue to bombard trench junctions and strong points in advance of the barrages, moving up and down communication trenches.
   Machine gun barrages will also be provided by 68th and 194th Machine Gun Companies on localities well in rear.

8. ~~Infantry will leave their trenches at Zero plus 2~~ and the assault of the Red Line will be carried through without halt as close up to the barrage as possible. The general rate of advance is calculated at 25 yards a minute. Troops from the reserve will move up to trenches vacated by assaulting Battalions.

9. The O.C. 69th Trench Mortar Battery will place two Stokes Guns under an officer at the disposal of each of the three front Battalions to cross No Man's Land and assist in the capture of Blue and Black Lines.

   One Stokes will be in position off WANGARATTA about I.29.d.10.90. and one near BERRY POST. These two guns will commence firing at Zero plus 2 on the East front and the support trenches of the SNOUT and on any machine gun positions which may be active.

   Headquarters 69th Trench Mortar Battery and reserve men and equipment will be in LARCH WOOD Tunnels.

10. The O.C. 69th Machine Gun Company will hold the following guns in readiness to advance and assist in consolidation:-

    (a) Two guns in VERRET RIDE to consolidate strong point at I.29.d.50.40.
    (b) Two guns in Australian Tunnels to consolidate front lip of new crater on HILL 60 at about I.29.c.90.00.
    (c) Two guns in LEEK TRENCH to advance to front lip of new CATERPILLAR Crater and consolidate about I.35.a.90.60.
    (d) Two guns near GRAND FLEET STREET to advance to I.35.a.40.10. and consolidate a strong point there.

    Advance parties will be sent forward behind the first wave of Infantry to select positions. The guns and teams will be brought up at discretion of the M.G. Officer i/c each party but as soon as practicable.

    Six guns will remain in defensive positions as follows:-

    (e) Two guns in WANGARATTA. One of these will enfilade the rear of the SNOUT from Zero to Zero plus 2. The other will be in reserve.
    (f) Two guns in the tunnels ready to take up normal positions in LARCH WOOD and Infantry Tunnel after explosion of the mines.
    (g) Two guns will be in normal positions C.6.(I.34.b.5.9.) and new L.10.(I.28.d.45.35.)

    Company Headquarters and two reserve guns and teams will be at S.P.9.

    O.C. 69th Machine Gun Company will arrange for the officers selected for (a), (b), (c) and (d) above to discuss details at an early date with Unit Commanders in whose area they will be operating.

11. Formations in attack etc.

    The assault up to the Blue Line will be made by 10th Duke of Wellington's Regt. on the Right, 8th Yorkshire Regt. in the centre and 11th West Yorkshire Regt. on left.

    There will be four waves of attack for each Battalion.

    The supporting companies will consolidate strong points in the German Second Line.

    Moppers Up will be provided from their companies for the German front line and communication trenches.

    Distance between lines 20 yards, between waves 50 yards and between companies 100 yards.

    Parties for carrying sufficient material for rapid consolidation of strong points and of the Blue Line will be detailed by O.C. Units.

12. O.C. 10th Duke of Wellington's Regt., will ensure that touch is obtained with 142nd Brigade at each important trench as soon as possible after the barrage lifts from it.

The O.C. 11th West Yorkshire Regt., will arrange for parties to be sent out to meet 70th Brigade patrols as soon as possible after reaching the following trenches :-

Approximate time :- IMMEDIATE TRENCH   Zero plus 12.
                         IMMEDIATE SUPPORT   Zero plus 20.
                         IMMEDIATE AVENUE   Zero plus 35.

13. Every platoon, every section, and as far as possible every man must be given a definite point to reach and work to do in each objective to be attacked.

Moppers up will be allotted exact areas to clear and must be given definite routes.

Lewis Gun Sections and Bomb sections will be allotted definite objects to reach and to convert into strong points as quickly as possible.

The determination to reach his personal objective and to consolidate it at all costs must be impressed on every man.

14. While the leading companies are attacking the trenches between the Red and Blue lines, the German Support line is to be rapidly consolidated by wiring strong points at trench junctions etc., and by posting Lewis Guns.

The following among other posts are to be made :-

I.35.c.10.90.
I.35.a.40.10.   (for machine gun)
I.35.a.50.40.
I.35.a.75.50.
I.35.a.90.60.   front lip of crater (for machine guns)
I.29.c.90.00.   front lip of crater (for machine guns)
I.29.d.50.40.   (for machine gun)
I.29.d.50.60.
I.29.d.80.50.

Lewis gun teams will move direct on all the above accompanied by bombers and carrying sufficient material to commence strong points at once. The machine guns will be brought up to relieve Lewis guns at the four places noted for them as soon as practicable. Reports will be sent to Battalion Commanders concerned and to Brigade H.Q. as soon as the machine guns are in position.

15. Four 4" Stokes Mortars under special Coy. R.E. will fire Thermite and White Phosphorous from the vicinity of WOOLLEY WALK against IMPACT RESERVE from Zero plus 5 minutes to Zero plus 15 minutes.

16. For the purpose of holding our line during the assault three Lewis gun sections of 9th Yorkshire Regt. will be attached to 10th West Riding Regt. during Y/Z night and will remain in position.

Three Lewis gun sections of battalion of 68th Brigade will similarly be attached to 11th West Yorkshire Regt. on Y/Z night.

O.C. 8th Yorkshire Regt. will detail from his own Battalion such troops as he considers necessary to hold his front line during the assault.

17. The capture of the third (Black) objective will be carried out by 9th Yorkshire Regt. on the Right and 12th Durham L.I. on the Left.
These will pass through the Blue Line at Zero plus 3 hours 40 minutes.
The Black Line is to be consolidated at once and strongly held, posts being pushed forward to cover consolidation.
One Battalion of 68th Brigade will remain in Brigade reserve.

18. Communication across No Man's Land will be provided as follows :-

    (a). From GRAND FLEET STREET.
    (b). From NOSRAC.
    (c). From SWIFT STREET TO IMMOVABLE ROW.
    (d). From ALIEN CRATER.

Of these (a) and (b) will be provided by 1st Australian Tunnelling Compnay, and (c) and (d) by R.E. and Pioneers.

19. R.E. and Pioneers will during Z/A night construct strong points for occupation by machine guns of 69th Machine Gun Company at

    (a). I.35.a.4.1.
    (b). The CATERPILLAR about I.35.b.6.0.

The strong point at I.29.d.5.4. will also be improved.

H.Q. 69th Inf.Bde.
May 24th, 1917.
B.M.S.437/16.

Capt.,
Brigade Major.
69th Infantry Brigade.

9th YORKSHIRE REGIMENT.

REPORT ON THE ATTACK ON BATTLE WOOD ON 7TH JUNE 1917.

The attack was made through the Blue Line at 6-50 a.m. in two lines in small columns in Artillery formation, "A" Coy on the Right, "C" Coy on the left, supported by "B" and "D" Coys respectively. About the first 200 yards the advance did not meet with very great resistance, and troops kept close up to our own barrage. After this the Undergrowth became increasingly thick and Snipers and Machine Gun fire caused many casualties. It was with great difficulty that touch was maintained with the troops on our flanks, and for some considerable time we were well in front of them and our advance was checked by a flanking fire. The Bn. was eventually forced to dig itself in on the Southern edge of the Wood owing to heavy M.Gun fire from emplacements just beyond our objective, which made further advance practically impossible. I am of the opinion that the objective allotted to this Bn. was situated on low ground in the very centre of a strong hostile position, and one which had been carefully organized for defensive purposes with concealed Machine Gun emplacements on the rising ground in front, and on our flanks. For reasons which are not clear to me these emplacements did not appear to have been dealt with by our Artillery. The arrangements previous to the attack were quite efficient so far as I am in a position to judge, but the Signalling communication during the attack was very unsatisfactory. I found it impossible to get in touch with Brigade by this means until 7 hours after the attack was launched, although every effort to do so was made on our part. The Artillery laison Officer did not report to me at all on the 7th inst., and although our own guns were consistently bombarding the position, we had just captured, it was impossible to get in touch with the Artillery in order to get them to lengthen their range. I would suggest that in future a series of coloured Very Lights be used for this purpose.

The enclosed reports from Coys make the situation on each flank more clear for the information of the G.O.C. If these could be returned to me I should be obliged.

16/6/17.

(sd) H.A.S.Prior. Lieut.Colonel.
Commanding 9th Yorkshire Regiment.

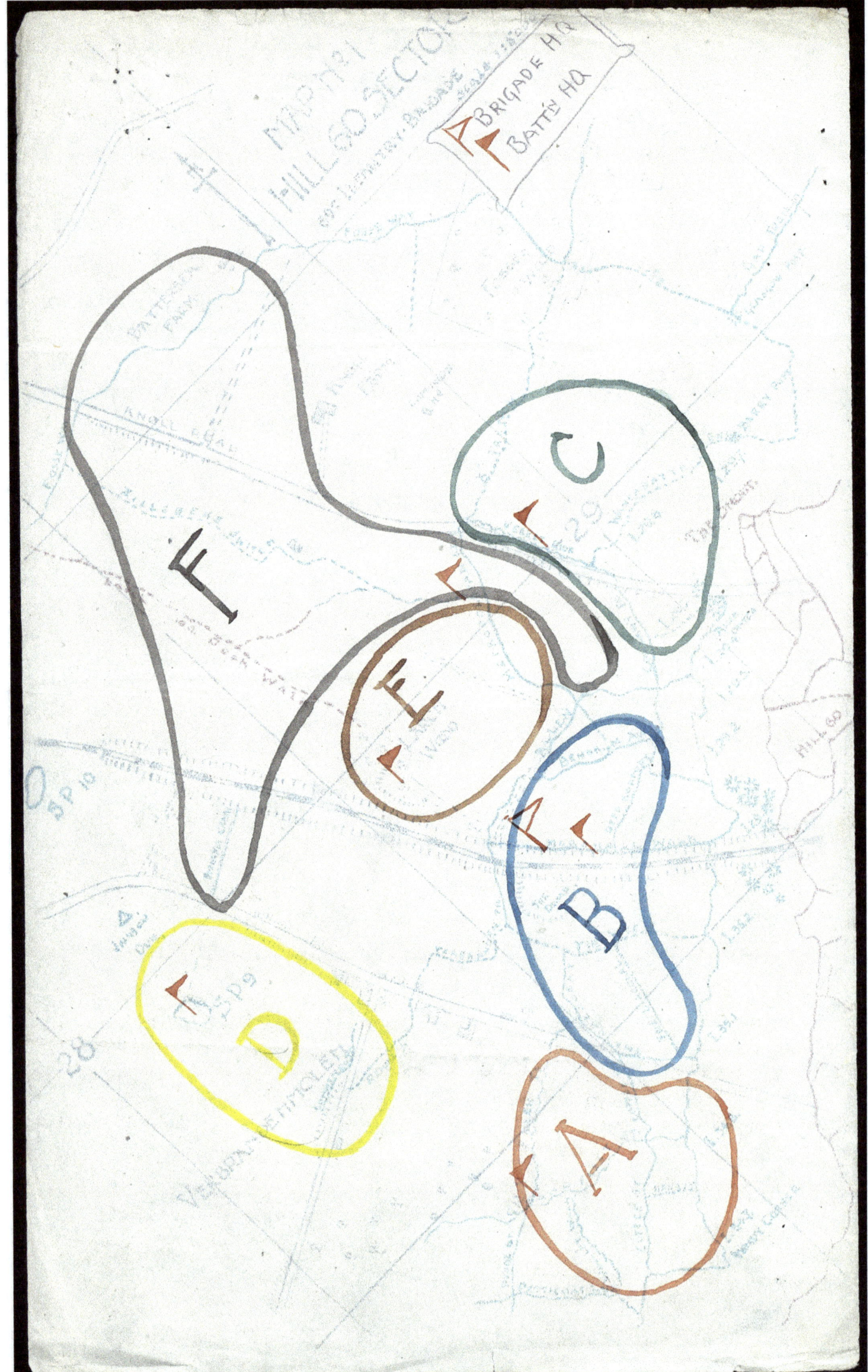

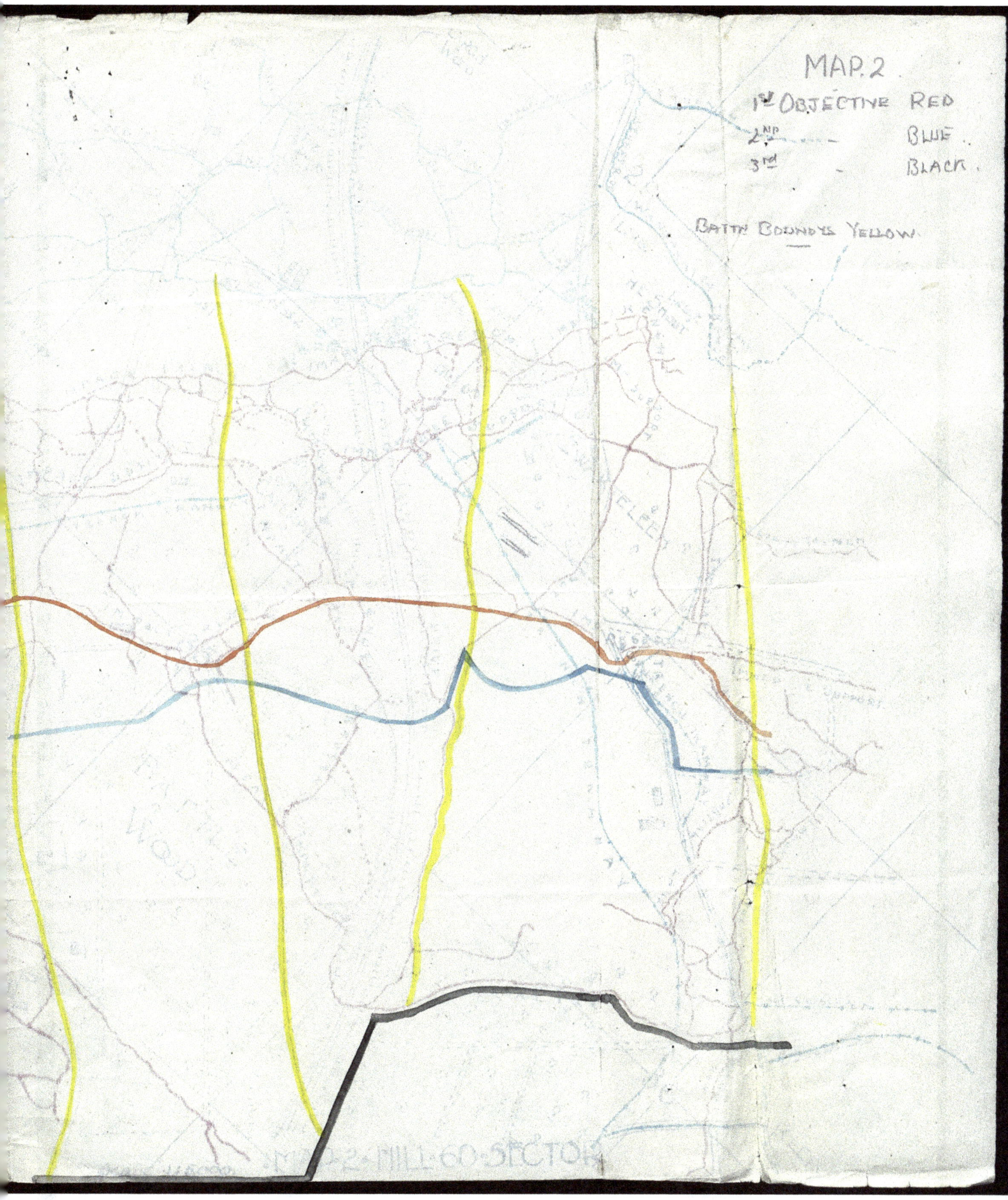

MAP. 2
1st OBJECTIVE RED
2nd — BLUE.
3rd — BLACK.

BATTN BOUND'YS YELLOW.

MAP 2. HILL 60 SECTOR

9th Yorkshire Regiment

Appendix I

"A" Copy No 3 69th Brigade "X" Scheme with Plans attached.

"B" Copy report of CO on operations in BATTLE WOOD

[signature] CAPT. & ADJT.
FOR O.C. 9TH YORKS REGT.

9th Yorkshire Regiment.

Appendix II

Date	Officers Killed	Officers Wounded	Other Ranks Killed	Other Ranks Wounded	Other Ranks Missing	Horses K	Horses W	Horses M	Mules K	Mules W	Mules M	Remarks
7.6.17	2/Lieut L.W. Knott	Capt. W.R. Gamble " H.J. Greenwood. Lieut. L.J. Bore R.H. Tolson. 2/Lieut. E.E. Knowles. " T.W. Scan " D.B. Abinghill " H.E. Robson. " R.T. Eustis " L. Read	67	178	9	9						Capt. W.R. Gamble subsequently died of wounds 14.6.17 2/Lt. E.E. Knowles subsequently died of wounds 9.6.17 2/Lt. T.W. Scan subsequently died of wounds 7.6.17
8.6.17			1	3	1							
9.6.17			1	2	1							
11.6.17			1	4	1							
12.6.17			1	2		1	3	1				
22.6.17			2	1								
23.6.17			1	1								
29.6.17				1								

O.C. 11th West Yorkshire Regt.
    8th Yorkshire Regt.
    9th Yorkshire Regt.
    10th West Riding Regt.
    69th Machine Gun Company.
    69th Trench Mortar Battery.

With reference to my B.M.S. 437/16 of the 25th inst. Attached please find the special maps referred to.

Please acknowledged receipt.

H.Q. 69th Inf. Bde.
May 27th, 1917.
B.M.S. 437/22.

Capt.,
Brigade Major.
69th Infantry Brigade.

WAR DIARY
or
INTELLIGENCE SUMMARY.
(Erase heading not required.)

Army Form C. 2118.

9 York R.

Vol 24

Place	Date	Hour	Summary of Events and Information	Remarks and references to Appendices
DICKEBUSH	1.7.17		In Brigade Reserve at DICKEBUSH. Under canvas. Fine weather.	
STEENVOORDE AREA	4.7.17		Entrained at OUDERDOM SIDING, detrained at GODEWAERSVELDE and marched to billets near STEENVOORDE and WINNIZEELE. Perfect weather.	
MIC MAC CAMP	11.7.17		Marched to GODEWAERSVELDE, entrained for OUDERDOM & they marched to MICMAC CAMP. Very hot day.	
HEDGE ST. TUNNELS	11.7.17		B & C Coys FHQ moved to HEDGE ST TUNNELS in relief of 2 Coys FHQ of 11th N.F.s	
"	12.7.17		B & C Coys relieved 2 Coys 10th N.F.s in front line. A & D Coys relieved 2 Coys 10th N.F.s – A in CANADA TRENCH – "D" in HEDGE ST. TUNNELS. 8th East Surreys on left of front – 8th Yorks. Regt. on right flank	For casualties see Appendix attached
"	16.7.17		To support on relief by 10th W. Riding R. dispositions as follows:- A Coy CANADA TRENCH. B Coy RUDKIN HOUSE, 'C' Coy METROPOLITAN LEFT, H.Q. 'D' Coy HEDGE ST. TUNNELS.	
"	19.7.17		Moved to front line in relief of 10th W.Riding Regt. and occupied position on on night 12.7.17 Relieved by 9th Royal Sussex Regt. and moved to MIC MAC CAMP. Relief hampered by hostile shell fire, causing a few casualties.	
MIC MAC CAMP	23.7.17			
BERTHEN AREA LA WATTINE OVERCOMP WESTBECOURT BOUVELINGHEM	23.7.17 26.7.17		Marched to BERTHEN AREA. Marched to Billets as per margin for training in TILQUES AREA.	
BOISDINGHEM ZUTOVE	30.7.17		H.Q, A, B & D Coys moved to Billets at BOISDINGHEM and ZUTOVE, 'C' Coy remaining at LA WATTINE. Training considerably hampered owing to bad weather.	

Appendix

9th Yorkshire Regiment

Date	Officers Killed	Officers Wounded	O.R. Killed	O.R. Wounded	O.R. Missing	Horses K	Horses W	Horses M	Mules K	Mules W	Mules M	Remarks
6.7.17 11.7.17		2/Lt H. Salmon (accidentally)		2								
13.7.17		2/Lt LS J Catton										
15.7.17				4								
18.7.17				8								
19.7.17				1							1	
20.7.17			6	3								
22.7.17				1	2							
TOTALS			6	20	2						1	

For O.C. 9th Yorks Regt.
Capt. & Adjt.

CONFIDENTIAL

Vol 25

9TH YORKSHIRE REGT.

WAR DIARY
Vol. 25

From August 1st 1917

To August 31st 1917

[signature]
CAPT & ADJT for
O.C. 9TH YORKSHIRE REGIMENT

Army Form C. 2118.

WAR DIARY
or
INTELLIGENCE SUMMARY.
(*Erase heading not required.*)

Instructions regarding War Diaries and Intelligence Summaries are contained in F. S. Regs., Part II. and the Staff Manual respectively. Title pages will be prepared in manuscript.

Place	Date	Hour	Summary of Events and Information	Remarks and references to Appendices
BOISDINGHEM to ZUTONE	1-8-17 to 9-8-17		In billets. Training in TILQUES AREA. Special attention being paid to attacking in open warfare. Good weather.	full
MOULLE	9.8.17	2.15 pm	Moved to billets at MOULLE by route march. Drenching rain en route. Special Training carried on in this area, particular attention being paid to musketry & open warfare. Perfect weather.	full
DALLINGTON CAMP	24.8.17	4.45 pm	Marched to WATTEN STATION and entrained there for ABEELE Station. Detrained there and proceeded to DALLINGTON CAMP, arrived there 5.15 am 25/8/17. Train very late leaving WATTEN STATION.	full
DICKEBUSCH	25.8.17	4.20 pm	Marched to ABEELE and entrained there for DICKEBUSCH arriving about 6.30 pm	full
do-	27.8.17		Reconnoitring parties proceeded to look over line INVERNESS COPSE to GLENCORSE WOOD preparatory to attack. 3 OR wounded when engaged on carrying party	full

— CONFIDENTIAL —

WAR DIARY Vol 26

of
9th Yorkshire Regt

From Sept 1st 1917 To Sept 30th 1917
(Volume 26)

A.B. Attins
Capt A/Adjt
9th Yorkshire Regt

Army Form C. 2118.

WAR DIARY
or
INTELLIGENCE SUMMARY.
(Erase heading not required.)

Instructions regarding War Diaries and Intelligence Summaries are contained in F. S. Regs., Part II. and the Staff Manual respectively. Title pages will be prepared in manuscript.

Place	Date	Hour	Summary of Events and Information	Remarks and references to Appendices
STEENVOORDE AREA	2.9.17		Moved to billets in STEENVOORDE AREA by Route March. Good weather.	
LEDERZEELE	3.9.17		Moved to billets in LEDERZEELE area by route march.	
— do —	4.9.17 to 12.9.17		Special training carried out in this area, particular attention being paid to the taking of Strong points. Good weather.	
STEENVOORDE AREA	13.9.17		Moved to billets in STEENVOORDE AREA by route march.	
WESTOUTRE	14.9.17		Moved to camp in WESTOUTRE AREA by route march.	
MICMAC AREA	16.9.17		Moved to No.4 Camp MICMAC AREA by route march.	
RAILWAY DUGOUTS	18.9.17		Moved up to RAILWAY DUGOUTS	Report Appendix A
	19.9.17 to 23.9.17		Engaged in Operations in the neighbourhood of INVERNESS COPSE as per appendix A attached	Casualties Appendix B
DICKEBUSCH AREA	24.9.17		Moved down to camp in the DICKEBUSCH AREA	
WESTOUTRE AREA	25.9.17		Moved to WOOD CAMP South, WESTOUTRE AREA by march-route.	
	26.9.17		Re-organising.	
STIRLING CASTLE	27.9.17		Moved up to STIRLING CASTLE via SCOTTISH WOOD	
	30.9.17		Moved up to front line.	

— CONFIDENTIAL —

WAR DIARY
OF
9TH YORKSHIRE REGT.

FROM 1ST OCTR. 1917 TO 31ST OCTR. 1917.
(VOLUME 27)

Capt. A/Adjt
9th Yorkshire Regt

Army Form C. 2118.

WAR DIARY
or
INTELLIGENCE SUMMARY.
(Erase heading not required.)

Instructions regarding War Diaries and Intelligence Summaries are contained in F.S. Regs., Part II. and the Staff Manual respectively. Title pages will be prepared in manuscript.

Place	Date	Hour	Summary of Events and Information	Remarks and references to Appendices
TRENCHES	1-10-17	4.30 a.m. 7.30 a.m. 11.0 a.m.	The Battalion, plus one Coy 10th Duke of Wellingtons, took over from 8th Yorks as follows:— "A" Coy in Support by CARLISLE FARM. — "D" Coy J.15.d.50.45 to REUTEL BEEK J.15.& 60.65 — "B" Coy REUTEL BEEK to JUT FARM J.16.c.10.20 — "D" Coy Duke of Wellington's JUT FARM J.16.c.10.20 to J.16.a.50.50 — "C" Coy remained in same billets. Very heavy barrage put up by enemy from 4.30 a.m. "C" Coy on our left attacked, heavy casualties faced. Communication between H.Q. and Coys very difficult. Relieved by 1st East Surrey Regt. Returned to STIRLING CASTLE for the night, afterwards at 11 a.m. proceeding back to	S.
RIDGE WOOD	2.10.17		RIDGE WOOD. 1st Duke of Cornwall's Light Infantry taking over vacated positions.	S.S.
BERTHEN AREA	3.10.17		Moved by buses to BERTHEN AREA. Weather, very good. 'B','C' and 'D' Coys billets far away from Bn. H.Q.	S.
— do —	4.10.17		Coys reorganising and cleaning up. News of "C" Coy better.	S.
— do —	5.10.17		Coys reorganising and refitting. Coys moved into billets nearer H.Q. Only 1 Officer and 10 men missing from "C" Coy.	S.S.
— do —	6.10.17		Weather still bad. Weather very unsettled and cold.	S.
— do —	7.10.17		Brigade Church Parade at 8th Yorks. Service conducted by Deputy Chaplain Gen. Bishop Guyne. Weather still bad.	S.
— do —	8.10.17		Training carried on by Coys in vicinity of billets. Weather still very cold and cheerless.	S.
WOOD CAMP S.	9.10.17		Sudden Move Order. Proceeded by buses to WOOD CAMP SOUTH. Temporarily attached to 70th Brigade.	S.R.

Army Form C. 2118.

WAR DIARY
or
INTELLIGENCE SUMMARY.
(Erase heading not required.)

SHEET 2.

Instructions regarding War Diaries and Intelligence Summaries are contained in F. S. Regs., Part II. and the Staff Manual respectively. Title pages will be prepared in manuscript.

Place	Date	Hour	Summary of Events and Information	Remarks and references to Appendices
No.1. AREA	10.10.17		Moved to No1 AREA H.30.c.3.3. Weather a little better. Camp very wet and muddy.	C.R.
BUND	11.10.17		C.O. and 2 Coy Commanders (A+B) went up to reconnoitre the line. Moved to ZILLEBEKE BUND in the afternoon. Battalion in Reserve.	C.R.
TRENCHES	13.10.17		Moved up to Front Line, relieving 8th York Lancs Regt. "A" and "B" Coys in Front Line. J.12.a.2.2. to J.6.c.2.2. "C" and "D" Coys in Support. HQrs at the BUTTE. Heavy rain.	C.R.
— do —	14.10.17		Support Coys rather badly shelled during preceeding night. Normal during day.	C.R.
— do —	15.10.17		Support Coys again heavily shelled. Trenches blown in and several casualties, including Captain H.E.H.Millar, M.C. Normal during day. O.C. & Adjt. 11th Sherwood Foresters came up to reconnoitre. One Coy Sherwood Foresters came up to SUPPORT LINE in evening. Weather fine.	C.R.
— do —	16.10.17		Relieved by 11th Sherwood Foresters at night. 3 Coys moving to Support at CLAPHAM JUNCTION. "B" Coy moved to T.H.Q. Weather fine.	C.R.
No.1. AREA	18.10.17		Afternoon, relieved by 10th Northumberland Fusiliers and moved down to Camp H.30.c.9.1. Weather fine.	C.R.
— do —	19.10.17		Billeting party sent to BOISDINGHEM. Coys. cleaning up, reorganising etc. At night party of Transport proceeded by road to BOISDINGHEM. Heavy rain in morning. Afternoon S.O.G. Divn. present Medal Ribbons.	C.R.
BOISDINGHEM	20.10.17		Bn. and remainder of Transport moved by train from DICKEBUSH to BOISDINGHEM, arriving at 9 p.m.	C.R.

Army Form C. 2118.

WAR DIARY
or
INTELLIGENCE SUMMARY.

SHEET 3. *(Erase heading not required.)*

Instructions regarding War Diaries and Intelligence Summaries are contained in F.S. Regs., Part II and the Staff Manual respectively. Title pages will be prepared in manuscript.

Place	Date	Hour	Summary of Events and Information	Remarks and references to Appendices
BOISDINGHEM	21.10.17		Coys cleaning up. Weather good.	
do	22.10.17 23.10.17		Training carried on by Coys. Weather good.	
do	25.10.17		"A" & "D" Coys on range. 90.6 presented 2 M.Cs, 2 D.C.Ms and 7 M.Ms.	
do	26.10.17		En route marched. Returned early owing to bad weather.	
do	27.10.17		Ceremonial parade in Morning	
do	28.10.17		Bn fired on Range.	
do	29.10.17		Brigade inspected by G.O.C. Divn. New draft of 203 arrived. Rather poor.	
do	30.10.17		Training carried on by Coys. Very wet.	
do	31.10.17		Brigade inspected by Commander-in-Chief. Splendid weather. For Casualties see appendix attached	

APPENDIX "A"

Short account of the action of the 9th Yorkshire Regiment. in the neighbourhood of INVERNESS COPSE September the 19th to 25th 1917.

The Bn. left MICMAC CAMP at 1.10 p.m. on the 18th inst and proceeded to RAILWAY DUGOUTS.

Headquarters, "A" and "B" Coy's remained here for the night of the 18/19th while "C" and "D" Coys after having been issued with Battle Stores proceeded at 5.30 p.m. to SANCTUARY WOOD where they dug themselves in. During the night of the 18/19th these latter Coys were heavily shelled with H.E. and Gas Shells and lost 12 casualties.

At 1 p.m. on the 19th inst H.Q. moved up to CLAPHAM JUNCTION under the MENIN ROAD and "A" and "B" Coys moved up to the vicinity of STIRLING CASTLE and SANCTUARY WOOD.

At 9.30 p.m. Coys commenced to move into their assembly positions ready for attack and all these positions were completed by 2 a.m. on the 20th inst.

At Zero (5.30 a.m. on the 20th) "A" and "D" left their assembly positions and advanced towards INVERNESS COPSE closely followed by "B" and "C" Coys. The morning was dark and there was a considerable mist. This combined with the dense clouds of smoke caused by our Artillery barrage rendered the question of keeping direction extremely difficult.

In spite of this and in spite of the fact that the ground over which they were advancing was pitted with shell holes and strewn with broken tree trunks and barbed wire, very little loss of direction occurred until the Bn. had advance about 150 to 200 yards into the Copse. Here according to arrangement a halt was called for about three quarters of an hour, troops taking advantage of shell holes and natural cover. Even in this early stage isolated instances of fighting occurred, individual Germans who had not been mopped up bombing our men from the rear where the enemy also fired a green S.O.S. Very Light.

During this paise troops were reorganised and the direction checked with the aid of compasses, while the men were in the best of spirits in spite of the heavt artillery and machine gun fire, sat in shell holes smoking German cigars calmly waiting for the advance.

At Zero plus 1 hour 2 minutes Coys commenced to move forward and it was while advancing from this position to the RED LINE that some of the heaviest fighting occurred. Numerous small parties of GERMANS remained in the wood in dugouts and shell holes, and many of these put up a strong resistance attacking our men with bombs and causing many casualties by machine gun and rifle fire.

All these parties were however successfully mopped up, at least 60 Germans being killed in the Copse. By this time however, the Bn. had suffered considerable casualties both from Germans in the Wood, from machine gun fire from Strong Point beyond, and from a hostile artillery barrage. Before reaching the RED LINE 8 out of 16 Coy Officers had already become casualties, including 2 of the Coy Commanders. In spite of this however, the men formed up well under the barrage ready to go forward to the assault at Zero plus 1 hour 28 minutes according to programme.

As was previously anticipated the main centres of German resistance were around the line of dugouts extending from the TOWER on the North, Southwards to the small pond by the MENIN Road. These dugouts had hardly suffered at all from our artillery barrage and around them the fighting varied considerably in intensity. Several hostile parties as soon as they recognised that they were outflanked abandoned their machine guns and weapons and came forward waving small white pieces of cloth which had obviously been prepared beforehand. Around several of the dugouts however, the fiercest hand-to-hand fighting occurred, the Germans holding out to the last and refusing to surrender. Our men here got well home with the bayonet and many Germans were killed both around the TOWER and in the actual passages of the dugouts themselves. In this part no fewer than 10 machine guns were captured, some in concrete emplacements others in open shell holes. Fifteen Flammenwerfer, Five Trench Howitzers and Four Trench Mortars were also taken in this vicinity.

While "A" and "D" Coys were thus engaged in mopping up these positions, "B" and "C" Coys passed through them and advanced towards the BLUE LINE. Each of these Coys had at this time only one Officer left and one of these had already been shot through the helmet and wounded in the hand. In spite of this, and notwithstanding the heavy losses, they had suffered earlier in the day both in N.C.Os and men, so thoroughly did each man know the individual task whoch had been allotted to him, that formations

(Sheet 2)

and direction still continued to be well maintained and each Section made independently for its own objective on the BLUE LINE, captured it, and commenced to consolidate it.

Although this work of consolidation was much hampered by the fire of enemy machine guns and snipers, the ground was soft and all men worked intensively so that by the time the barrage moved forward to the GREEN LINE every man had provided himself with good cover. While this consolidation was in progress an excellent target presented itself on our left front where a large number of the enemy were observed to be retiring over the Ridge. Lewis Gun and rifle fire was immediately brought to bear on these and it is thought that a number of casualties were inflicted on the enemy.

In the meanwhile Bn.H.Q. had moved up to an advanced position in the German Aid Post just South of the MENIN Road at 9.15 a.m.

Throughout the remainder of the day the positions occupied were improved and consolidated and stores brought up, so that when a heavy barrage was opened by the enemy during the afternoon and evening in conjunction with the counter-attacks of the TOWER HAMLETS RIDGE very few casualties occurred.

On the morning of the 21st it was found advisable to thin out the posts in the vicinity of the REUTELBEEK where the ground was very marshy, and to transfer these men to better positions on the right of the BLUE LINE. Our positions were shelled by the enemy througout the day but with particular intensity during the afternoon and evening.

On the afternoon of the 22nd as a result of the heavy casualties inflicted on other Battalions of the Brigade the 9th Yorkshire Regt. was called upon to take over a portion of the GREEN LINE. "B" and "C" Coys took over the positions previously occupied by "A" and "D" Coys. "A" Coy took over the portion of the front line North of the REUTELBEEK Road from the Australians. "D" Coy took over a portion of the front line South of the REUTELBEEK from the 8th Yorkshire Regt. Battalion Headquarters moved to dugout just South of the TOWER.

On the night of the 23/24th "A" Coy were relieved by the 8th Yorks & Lancs Regt and moved to JACKDAW CRATERS.

On the night of the 24/25th Bn.H.Q. and "C" Coy were relieved by Bn. H.Q. and "C" Coy of the 2/5th Bn.Worcester Regt. "D" and "B" Coys were relieved by 2 Coys of the 4th Bn.Kings Liverpool Regt.

The Bn. on relief being complete at 8.20 p.m. on the 24th inst moved to Camp Area No.1 near DICKEBUSH.

26/9/17.   (sd) R.S.HART, Lieut.Colonel.
Commanding 9th.Bn.Yorkshire Regiment.

APPENDIX "B"

Casualties during September 1917.

Date.	OFFICERS. Killed.	Wounded.	Missing.	O.RANKS. Killed.	Wnd.	Missing
16/9/17.	-	-	-	-	1	-
18/9/17.	-	-	-	-	1※	-
19/9/17.	-	-	-	6	10	-
20/9/17.	Lt. N. Groom. 2/Lt. H.J. Bunker. " L. Nicholson. " R.M. Matthews.	Capt. G.N. Hunnybun. " D.W. Maude. Lt. H. Duncalfe. 2/Lt. I.G. Evans. " R. Wood. " B. Wahl.	-	19	139	28
21/9/17.	-	-	-	5	21	1
22/9/17.	-	-	-	2	18	-
23/9/17.	-	-	-	3	5	-
24/9/17.	-	-	-	3	3	-
27/9/17.	-	-	-	1	1	1
28/9/17.	-	-	-	-	4	1
30/9/17.	-	-	-	-	7	-

※ Self-inflicted.

www.ingramcontent.com/pod-product-compliance
Lightning Source LLC
Chambersburg PA
CBHW081555160426
43191CB00011B/1941